MAKE TIME FOR *joy*

Other Books by Linda Evans Shepherd

Praying God's Promises

Empowered for Purpose

Called to Pray

How to Pray in Times of Stress

When You Don't Know What to Pray

How to Pray When You Need a Miracle

Experiencing God's Presence

When You Need to Move a Mountain

Praying through Hard Times

Praying through Every Emotion

Prayers for Every Need

Novels

The Potluck Club

The Potluck Club

The Potluck Club—Trouble's Brewing

The Potluck Club—Takes the Cake

The Potluck Catering Club

The Secret's in the Sauce

A Taste of Fame

Bake Until Golden

Scripture-Powered Prayers to Brighten Your Day

LINDA EVANS SHEPHERD

a division of Baker Publishing Group
Grand Rapids, Michigan

Published by Revell
a division of Baker Publishing Group
PO Box 6287, Grand Rapids, MI 49516-6287
www.revellbooks.com

Printed in the United States of America

Library of Congress Cataloging-in-Publication Data
Names: Shepherd, Linda E., 1957– author.
Title: Make time for joy : scripture-powered prayers to brighten your day / Linda Evans Shepherd.
Description: Grand Rapids, MI : Revell, a division of Baker Publishing Group, [2023] | Includes bibliographical references.
Identifiers: LCCN 2022014420 | ISBN 9780800740917 (cloth) | ISBN 9781493439836 (ebook)
Subjects: LCSH: Joy—Biblical teaching—Miscellanea. | Joy—Religious aspects—Christianity—Miscellanea. | Prayers.
Classification: LCC BV4647.J68 S54 2023 | DDC 242—dc23/eng/20220815
LC record available at https://lccn.loc.gov/2022014420

Published in association with Books & Such Literary Management, www.booksandsuch.com.

Baker Publishing Group publications use paper produced from sustainable forestry practices and post-consumer waste whenever possible.

23 24 25 26 27 28 29 7 6 5 4 3 2 1

CONTENTS

RECLAIMING JOY

LIVING INTO JOY

WORSHIP INTO JOY

To my dear friend and editor, Vicki Crumpton.
It has been a joy to walk with you through
the pages of my books. May the joy of
the Lord continually bless you.

INTRODUCTION

> You will show me the way of life. Being with You is to be full of joy. In Your right hand there is happiness forever.
>
> Psalm 16:11 NLV

Have you ever wanted a heart infused with joy no matter your circumstances? Then I have good news! The book you're holding contains a tried-and-true road map that will lead you straight to the treasure of a joyful heart.

These easy directions will guide you with God's Word and prayer so you can refuel and avoid major breakdowns.

I must warn you that the road to happiness may have a few detours, but praying God's promises will get you back on track.

If you're ready to take this journey, you'll soon discover that trusting God is the best path to joy that endures.

Will you take this adventure with me? I hope you'll say yes. For living your life with a joyful heart is the best way to steer clear of a crushed spirit.

Let's start our road trip together by reading the Scripture below, then praying a promise that God wants us to take to heart.

> I, the Lord your God, hold your right hand
> and say to you, "Don't be afraid; I will help you." (Isa. 41:13 GW)

Dear Lord,

I am ready to leave my state of despair, depression, and misery behind. I am ready to take this journey to a joyful heart with You. For You have opened the prison door that has kept me in bondage to my problems. You've reached Your hand into my cell and pulled me to freedom!

Though I believed sadness was my final destination, I now know I can journey past sadness into joy with You.

As I step toward You, I realize freedom awaits me and my emotions lift.

Even if I should stumble, I know I can trust You to lift me up and set me back on the road to joy.

Thank You, Lord!

In the name of Jesus, amen.

HOW TO USE THIS BOOK

You can read this book as a daily devotional, or you can consult the table of contents to find prayers you need right now. As you pray through this book, you'll discover that the prayers, like the one in the introduction, are a paraphrase of the accompanying Scripture passages. This is by design because there is such anointing and breakthrough when you pray God's Word back to Him.

God's Word is alive and filled with power and can take you into a state of joy. Praying God's Word gives you confidence that you are not only praying in His will but also agreeing with and activating His promises to you. Be sure to linger over the Scripture passages that go with each prayer because God's Word is the source of transforming power.

When you find a Scripture passage that speaks to you, read it again. Then use that passage to craft a prayer of your own. This is a way to continue in prayer and experience God's presence, which will lead you to joy.

When you find a prayer that has deep meaning to you, bookmark it and pray the prayer often. Consider meditating on and even memorizing the Scripture passages that accompany it so you can recall God's Word whenever you need it.

Don't be afraid to read prayers you don't relate to in the moment, because the moment may come when you will find the joy those prayers provide.

Be sure to keep an extra copy of *Make Time for Joy* on hand so you always have one to give to a friend or loved one.

God bless you as you travel to your new state of joy.

joy BUILDERS

Rejoice in the Lord always. Again I will say, rejoice!

Philippians 4:4 NKJV

I choose joy. . . . I will invite my God to be the God of circumstance. I will refuse the temptation to be cynical . . . the tool of the lazy thinker. I will refuse to see people as anything less than human beings, created by God. I will refuse to see any problem as anything less than an opportunity to see God.

Max Lucado

ABUNDANT LIFE

Dear Lord,

You've seen my shortcomings, which makes me wonder why You don't give up on me. But I forget who You are, a God who never fails, a God who never falls short. You are the God of love. Forgive me for misjudging Your love for me. You don't base Your love on how close to perfection I can come; You base Your love for me on who You are. You love me even when I don't deserve it.

Despite all my shortcomings, You give me Your grace. How grateful I am that You are not set to kill or destroy me. Instead, You fill me with overflowing abundance and grant me a life filled with joy.

You always deal with my shortcomings with grace and provide blessings for my every moment, even when I'm too blind to see Your gifts.

I praise You for who You are, the Eternal One who created me. You promise never to leave me as You lead me in the way I should go.

When I feel worthless, of no use to anyone, there You are, nourishing me with hope and strength.

I will grow in Your tender care as my roots grow deep in You. For this reason, I will be joyful. Because of Your love, my joy will be eternal like an ever-flowing spring.

Thank You, Lord.

The thief approaches with malicious intent, looking to steal, slaughter, and destroy; I came to give life with joy and abundance.

John 10:10 VOICE

And God is able to make all grace overflow to you, so that by always having enough of everything, you may overflow in every good work.

2 Corinthians 9:8 TLV

The Eternal One will never leave you;
He will lead you in the way that you should go.
When you feel dried up and worthless,
God will nourish you and give you strength.
And you will grow like a garden lovingly tended;
you will be like a spring whose water never runs out.

Isaiah 58:11 VOICE

CHOOSING JOY

Dear Lord,

I can hold on to my joy when trouble appears because You are my hope. Difficulties are opportunities for hope to burst forth in me because my troubles only serve to sharpen my focus on You. I stay in Your presence because Your name is always on my lips.

Therefore, I don't need to hide when troubles and hardships come searching for me. As difficult as they may be, when I learn to embrace them, I find Your hidden joy. That's when my faith blossoms and I learn to endure with true patience. This process equips me to race toward the finish line You have set before me. When I step into victory with You, I am not only joyful but mature, complete, and filled with satisfaction.

For in You, oh Lord, my heart rejoices, as I trust in Your holy name.

I've never once seen You, but I love You just the same. Even though I can't see You now, I'm putting my trust in You. This whole process of trusting You gives me joy so great that words cannot explain how wonderful I feel.

Thank You, Lord.

Let your hope keep you joyful, be patient in your troubles, and pray at all times.

Romans 12:12 GNT

Don't run from tests and hardships, brothers and sisters. As difficult as they are, you will ultimately find joy in them; if you embrace them, your faith will blossom under pressure and teach you true patience as you endure. And true patience brought on by endurance will equip you to complete the long journey and cross the finish line—mature, complete, and wanting nothing.

James 1:2–4 VOICE

In him our hearts rejoice,
for we trust in his holy name.

Psalm 33:21 NLT

You have never seen Him but you love Him. You cannot see Him now but you are putting your trust in Him. And you have joy so great that words cannot tell about it.

1 Peter 1:8 NLV

CONTENTMENT

Dear Lord,

Thank You for the gift of contentment, which You wrap around me like a blanket of love. You keep me in perfect peace whenever I remember to put my trust fully in You.

Trusting in You is a better bet than trusting in money. It's funny how money has a way of disappearing, but You never disappear. This truth has shown me that it's better to have You, my Provider, than money in the bank. For You always take care of me. You have promised me that You will never leave or abandon me.

Riches won't give me contentment, but when I am in You, I can find contentment even when I'm flat broke.

In fact, You are my secret to contentment. Whether I am full of food or go to bed hungry, I know I can trust in You because You will give me not only strength to endure but the ability to overcome.

The good news is that You are walking with me on a path that leads to a beautiful life. As we talk together, You bring me true joy and contentment because the pleasures of knowing You are never-ending.

Rich or poor, I am blessed.

Thank You, Lord.

You will keep in perfect peace
 those whose minds are steadfast,
 because they trust in you.

Isaiah 26:3 NIV

Don't love money. Be happy with what you have because God has said, "I will never abandon you or leave you."

Hebrews 13:5 GW

I am not saying this because I am in need, for I have learned to be content whatever the circumstances. I know what it is to be in need, and I know what it is to have plenty. I have learned the secret of being content in any and every situation, whether well fed or hungry, whether living in plenty or in want. I can do all this through him who gives me strength.

Philippians 4:11–13 NIV

You direct me on the path that leads to a beautiful life.
 As I walk with You, the pleasures are never-ending,
 and I know true joy and contentment.

Psalm 16:11 VOICE

COUNTING BLESSINGS

Dear Lord,

I sing with joy knowing You have riches to meet my every need, a supply that never runs out or leaves me in lack. As I look back at my past, I can see that You've always been my Provider. There were times when I didn't have everything I wanted, but You always gave me everything I needed.

And as a breathtaking bonus, You wrapped me in the righteousness of Jesus in order to cover my filthy rags stained with sin. This plan was the only way that You, a holy God, could walk with me, a fallen sinner. Thank You, Lord, that You've poured every spiritual blessing on me, blessings of love, joy, peace, and forgiveness, straight from heaven.

Your blessings make it easy for me to trust You because You have planted me like a green tree by a babbling brook. Because I am constantly refreshed by pools of the deep water of Your love, the heat will never shrivel my roots. My leaves will never wilt but will remain fresh and green as I serve You by bearing the fruit of love as a gift to You and to those You have put in my life.

You bless and protect me. You smile on me and are always gracious. You show me favor and give me Your peace.

Thank You, Lord.

And my God will meet all your needs according to the riches of his glory in Christ Jesus.

Philippians 4:19 NIV

Blessed be God, the Father of our Lord Jesus the Anointed One, who grants us every spiritual blessing in these heavenly realms where we live in the Anointed—not because of anything we have done, but because of what He has done for us.

Ephesians 1:3 VOICE

Blessed is the man who trusts in the LORD,
whose trust is the LORD.
He is like a tree planted by water,
that sends out its roots by the stream,
and does not fear when heat comes,
for its leaves remain green,
and is not anxious in the year of drought,
for it does not cease to bear fruit.

Jeremiah 17:7–8 ESV

May the LORD bless you
and protect you.
May the LORD smile on you
and be gracious to you.
May the LORD show you his favor
and give you his peace.

Numbers 6:24–26 NLT

EXPRESSING YOUR JOY

Dear Lord,

I shout for joy to You, for You are the Lord of all the earth. I will rejoice in You now and always because knowing that You, the Almighty, love me and know my name is too wonderful for words.

You give me so many everyday miracles, like the fact that I woke up again this morning. I'm grateful to be alive, and alive in You. For this is the day that You have made, and I invite You to share it with me. Guide me, protect me, bless me as we move through these precious hours together. How can I not express my joy to You? For I'm delighted that You are sharing all my moments with me.

There are so many reasons to delight in You, including the miracle that You allow me to dwell in You and Your safety.

Let me sing joyful praise to You forever. Spread Your protection over me so that I will be filled with more joy than I ever thought possible.

In the past, I missed out by hesitating to come to You with my prayer requests. I find it amazing that You invite me to ask for whatever is on my heart. So I ask now, knowing that You hear my requests and that I will receive wonderful blessings from You.

My joy is full.

Thank You, Lord.

Shout for joy to the LORD, all the earth.

Psalm 100:1 NIV

Rejoice in the Lord always. Again I will say, rejoice!

Philippians 4:4 NKJV

This is the day the LORD has made.
Let's rejoice and be glad today!

Psalm 118:24 GW

But let all who take refuge in you rejoice;
let them sing joyful praises forever.
Spread your protection over them,
that all who love your name may be filled with joy.

Psalm 5:11 NLT

Until now you have asked nothing in My name. Ask, and you will receive, that your joy may be full.

John 16:24 NKJV

GOD'S CARE

Dear Lord,

I will not fear or be dismayed, for You are my God. You will strengthen me. You will help me and hold my hand with Your righteous right hand.

You have said that You will watch over me and guide me along the best paths. You remind me that when I face a stormy sea, You will be with me, with unsinkable calm.

You tell me that even when I'm in the middle of a raging river, I will not be swept away.

You promise that if I'm walking through fire, I won't feel the flames as long as I keep on walking forward with You.

Jesus told a story about the birds that reminds me of Your care. He described how the birds don't plant, harvest, or store up crops, yet You, precious Lord, feed them through Your abundance. If You take care of the birds, You will surely take care of me.

Because You care for me, I will stop trying to carry all my burdens by myself. It's time that I hand them over to You. My burdens are now Your problem because I lay them all at Your feet. I know You will resolve them better than I ever could, and so, with joy, I trust You with these problems and the problem-people who try to block my way. I put these disrupters in Your hands so You can turn all my cares into blessings.

Thank You, Lord.

Fear not, for I am with you;
  be not dismayed, for I am your God;
I will strengthen you, I will help you,
  I will uphold you with my righteous right hand.

Isaiah 41:10 ESV

The Lord says, "I will guide you along the best pathway
  for your life.
  I will advise you and watch over you."

Psalm 32:8 NLT

When you face stormy seas I will be there with you with
  endurance and calm;
  you will not be engulfed in raging rivers.
If it seems like you're walking through fire with flames
  licking at your limbs,
  keep going; you won't be burned.

Isaiah 43:2 VOICE

Look at the birds. They don't plant, harvest, or gather the harvest into barns. Yet, your heavenly Father feeds them. Aren't you worth more than they?

Matthew 6:26 GW

Since God cares for you, let Him carry all your burdens and worries.

1 Peter 5:7 VOICE

GOD'S COMFORT

Dear Lord,

There is a secret to comfort and that secret starts with love—Your love for others, flowing through me. The secret behind this miracle is Christ Himself. Christ is the One who loved me first, the One whose love flows through me and into those You have put into my life.

This is a secret that money can't buy. The secret that You love me so much, You promise that no matter my mistakes, distress, or heartache, You will never leave me or abandon me.

One thing I look forward to in times of grief is that You are there to comfort me. How happy I am when You spread Your comfort over my broken heart.

I praise You with joy, God the Father of our Lord Jesus, the Father of all compassion and the God of all comfort. You comfort me in my troubles so I can comfort others in their troubles with the same comfort You used to comfort me.

As the shadows of death's darkness fall over my life, I will not give in to fear. Because You are with me, even in dark times. You cut through the darkness with the light of Your guidance and protection.

How Your unfailing love comforts me, just as You promised. Thank You, Lord.

May their hearts be given comfort. May they be brought close together in Christian love. May they be rich in understanding and know God's secret. It is Christ Himself.

Colossians 2:2 NLV

Don't love money. Be happy with what you have because God has said, "I will never abandon you or leave you."

Hebrews 13:5 GW

Those who have sorrow are happy, because they will be comforted.

Matthew 5:4 NLV

Praise be to the God and Father of our Lord Jesus Christ, the Father of compassion and the God of all comfort, who comforts us in all our troubles, so that we can comfort those in any trouble with the comfort we ourselves receive from God.

2 Corinthians 1:3–4 NIV

Even in the unending shadows of death's darkness,
I am not overcome by fear.
Because You are with me in those dark moments,
near with Your protection and guidance,
I am comforted.

Psalm 23:4 VOICE

Now let your unfailing love comfort me,
just as you promised me, your servant.

Psalm 119:76 NLT

GOD'S DIRECTION

Dear Lord,

Though I try to look toward my future, I have no idea what's in store and so I worry. I worry until I realize You've already created a plan filled with good, not disaster. You've written my future and filled it with hope.

To know You care about my life is so comforting. It's yet another reason to trust You with all my heart. I submit to your plan because I know I can trust that You will put me on the right path.

As we journey together, help my heart to be right with You so that I will stay strong and on task. May You be pleased with my actions and attitudes as we walk together all the days of my life.

When I trip, You stop me from falling on my face because You catch me with Your strong hands. Not only do You show me the way to go, You inspire me with the goals that You Yourself help me reach.

You even use my missteps to teach me lessons that will keep me on the path You've set for me. You work out all things because I'm called according to Your purpose. What joy I feel that the details of my life matter to You.

Thank You, Lord.

"For I know the plans I have for you," says the LORD. "They are plans for good and not for disaster, to give you a future and a hope."

Jeremiah 29:11 NLT

Trust in the LORD with all your heart
and lean not on your own understanding;
in all your ways submit to him,
and he will make your paths straight.

Proverbs 3:5–6 NIV

If you are right with God, He strengthens you for the journey;
the Eternal will be pleased with your life.
And even though you trip up, you will not fall on your face
because He holds you by the hand.

Psalm 37:23–24 VOICE

A person may plan his own journey,
but the LORD directs his steps.

Proverbs 16:9 GW

And we know that all things work together for good to those who love God, to those who are the called according to His purpose.

Romans 8:28 NKJV

GOD'S LOVE

Dear Lord,

You are the focus of my life, the Mighty One who saves me. You celebrate me with gladness. How amazing that You quiet me with Your love and rejoice over me with singing.

Your loving-kindness spreads to the heavens, for You are as faithful as the sky is high. Your righteousness and goodness loom higher than the mountaintops, and Your love for me is as deep as the sea. You keep me and all You have made safe. Your loving-kindness is my treasure, and my family and I nestle in the shadow of Your wings.

What joy to know how much You love me. This knowledge allows me to trust in You, for You are love. You have allowed Your love to dwell in my heart as I live in You and You live in me.

This is possible because You loved me so much that You gave Your only begotten Son, Jesus, to die for my sins, to take my punishment. Through Your power, He rose from the dead and is alive today. I believe and trust in Him, which means I will never perish but will have everlasting life.

Thank You, Lord.

The LORD your God is in your midst,
a mighty one who will save;
he will rejoice over you with gladness;
he will quiet you by his love;
he will exult over you with loud singing.

Zephaniah 3:17 ESV

O Lord, Your loving-kindness goes to the heavens. You are as faithful as the sky is high. You are as right and good as mountains are big. You are as fair when You judge as a sea is deep. O Lord, You keep safe both man and animal. Of what great worth is Your loving-kindness, O God! The children of men come and are safe in the shadow of Your wings.

Psalm 36:5–7 NLV

We know how much God loves us, and we have put our trust in his love. God is love, and all who live in love live in God, and God lives in them.

1 John 4:16 NLT

For God so [greatly] loved and dearly prized the world, that He [even] gave His [One and] only begotten Son, so that whoever believes and trusts in Him [as Savior] shall not perish, but have eternal life.

John 3:16 AMP

GOD'S UNDERSTANDING

Dear Lord,

I sometimes feel as though I'm ignorant of who You are! Who can tell me? Who understands Your greatness? For You are the Lord, the everlasting God, the Creator of all the earth. You never grow weak or weary. No one can measure the depths of Your genius or understanding. For Your riches, wisdom, and knowledge are so deep. Mystery shrouds Your thoughts, and there is no one who can know all Your secrets. Who could be Your mentor? Who could know Your mind?

But this I do know: You can see into my heart, and You know my thoughts through Your Spirit that dwells in me. In this same way, the Spirit knows Your thoughts of love toward me.

You know everything about me. You know when I sit or when I rise. You know my every thought. You know where I go and when I rest; You know all my ways. You know me so completely that You perceive what I will say even before I speak. You surround me with Yourself while You rest Your hand on me. Your complete knowledge of me is beyond my understanding.

Yet, despite what you know about me, You love me.

Despite my failures, You approve me to be in Your presence because of the work of Jesus.

What joy in knowing I'm known and loved by You.

What joy in knowing that You understand me and are on my side.

Thank You, Lord.

Have you never heard?
Have you never understood?
The Lord is the everlasting God,
the Creator of all the earth.
He never grows weak or weary.
No one can measure the depths of his understanding.

Isaiah 40:28 NLT

God's riches, wisdom, and knowledge are so deep! They are as mysterious as his judgments, and they are as hard to track as his paths!

Who has known the Lord's mind?
Or who has been his mentor?

Romans 11:33–34 CEB

Who can see into a man's heart and know his thoughts? Only the spirit that dwells within the man. In the same way, the thoughts of God are known only by His Spirit.

1 Corinthians 2:11 VOICE

You have searched me, Lord,
and you know me.
You know when I sit and when I rise;
you perceive my thoughts from afar.
You discern my going out and my lying down;
you are familiar with all my ways.
Before a word is on my tongue
you, Lord, know it completely.
You hem me in behind and before,
and you lay your hand upon me.
Such knowledge is too wonderful for me,
too lofty for me to attain.

Psalm 139:1–6 NIV

OUR LOVE

Dear Lord,

Because of Your love for me, I don't need to live in fear of Your punishment. You have replaced my fear of punishment with Your perfect love. I try my best to love You back. You graciously receive my love and cover all imperfection with Your glory. I will stay in Your love because Your love binds everything together in perfect harmony.

Your Spirit gives me the fruit of Your love along with joy, peace, patience, kindness, goodness, faithfulness, gentleness, and self-control. These gifts from Your loving Spirit are blessings wherever I spend them, gifts that are never turned away.

You even ask me to love others, to be kind, to think of how they are feeling, and to forgive. You ask me to forgive others not because the people in my life necessarily deserve forgiveness but because You have forgiven me when I didn't deserve it, through the death of Jesus on the cross.

The thing that's most important to You, more than sacrifices or offerings, is that I love You with all my heart and soul and mind and strength. You ask that I love others the same way I love myself.

What joy to serve You in love.

Thank You, Lord.

No fear exists where his love is. Rather, perfect love gets rid of fear, because fear involves punishment. The person who lives in fear doesn't have perfect love.

1 John 4:18 GW

And above all these put on love, which binds everything together in perfect harmony.

Colossians 3:14 ESV

But the fruit of the Spirit is love, joy, peace, forbearance, kindness, goodness, faithfulness, gentleness and self-control. Against such things there is no law.

Galatians 5:22–23 NIV

You must be kind to each other. Think of the other person. Forgive other people just as God forgave you because of Christ's death on the cross.

Ephesians 4:32 NLV

And to love God with all our heart and soul and mind and strength and to love our neighbors as ourselves are more important than any burnt offering or sacrifice we could ever give.

Mark 12:33 VOICE

PEACE

Dear Lord,

What would it look like if I made peace my priority instead of allowing my temper to flame whenever I don't get my way?

Instead of embracing what I want and how I want it, what if I submit my own selfish desires to You and ask for Your help? What if, through Your power, I make peace one of my top priorities? When I'm at peace with You, with others, and even with myself, I will be filled with joy. The bonus is that everyone will know I belong to You.

I need Your peace in every way. For peace has beautiful benefits because when I learn to trust You, You allow me to sleep soundly. You even keep my worries at bay so I can rest and be safe.

When I let my human nature control me, it turns out that I'm dancing with death. Instead of performing this deadly tap dance, I ask to be controlled by Your Spirit, who turns the dance into a lovely waltz that swirls with life and peace.

You have shared Your secrets of peace in Your Word so I can have joy. Your peace is with me even when I find myself in trouble. Because I can have Your peace in any circumstance I might face, I'm greatly cheered! You gave me this peace when You overcame the world.

Thank You, Lord.

Blessed are those who make peace.
They will be called God's children.

Matthew 5:9 GW

May the Lord of peace give you his peace at all times and in every way. The Lord be with all of you.

2 Thessalonians 3:16 GW

Tonight I will sleep securely on a bed of peace
because I trust You, You alone, O Eternal One, will keep me safe.

Psalm 4:8 VOICE

To be controlled by human nature results in death; to be controlled by the Spirit results in life and peace.

Romans 8:6 GNT

I've told you this so that my peace will be with you. In the world you'll have trouble. But cheer up! I have overcome the world.

John 16:33 GW

PROBLEMS INTO MIRACLES

Dear Lord,

Knowing You and Your love is greater than a payday. Knowing that You can turn my problems into blessings is a stunning bonus.

This means that whenever I walk into the middle of trouble, You don't hide from me; instead, as I trust You, You show up with dividends. For my trust turns into faith as You prove that You can transform any trouble into a blessing designed for my benefit. You even guard my life from my enemies.

Your reach is never too short, for time and again, You reach down to save me with Your righteous hand.

It's no secret that You are the One who delivers me. You—the Eternal God, the Lord—save me from the grip of death.

You are the One who turns my difficulties into joy not only because I love You but because You've chosen me to live with purpose—a purpose You planned from the beginning of time.

Your strength fills me as I sing to You. I will continue to praise You at the start of each new day, brightening the dawn with joyful song because You continue to show me mercy.

You are my safe place, my stronghold where I can rest in times of trouble.

Thank You, Lord.

Even though I walk into the middle of trouble,
you guard my life against the anger of my enemies.
You stretch out your hand,
and your right hand saves me.

Psalm 138:7 GW

We know our God is the God who delivers us,
and the Eternal, the Lord, is the One who saves us
from the grip of death.

Psalm 68:20 VOICE

We know that God makes all things work together for the good of those who love Him and are chosen to be a part of His plan.

Romans 8:28 NLV

But I will sing about your strength.
In the morning I will joyfully sing about your mercy.
You have been my stronghold
and a place of safety in times of trouble.

Psalm 59:16 GW

REFRESHING IN THE WORD

Dear Lord,

As I believe in Your Word that reveals Your Son, Jesus, a miracle happens. Rivers of living water flow deep from within my soul. This is the same living water Jesus offered the woman at the well when He revealed to her that He was the long-awaited Messiah.

The miracle is that because Your Word has become alive in me, my soul will never thirst.

For this message of Christ is rich and fills my life with joy! I will teach this Word and the wisdom that goes with it so that others can share in my joy.

The beauty of Your Word causes my heart to sing to You with hymns and spiritual songs because my heart is thankful.

Your Word will always be a light for my feet and a light to my path because it shows me the way to Jesus.

How joyful I am when I hear and obey Your Word. Jesus explained that if I remain in Him and in His Word, I can ask whatever I wish, and You will do it for me.

What a wonderful promise, a promise I activate with my prayer requests that I lift to You now.

Thank You, Lord.

As Scripture says, "Streams of living water will flow from deep within the person who believes in me."

John 7:38 GW

Let the message about Christ, in all its richness, fill your lives. Teach and counsel each other with all the wisdom he gives. Sing psalms and hymns and spiritual songs to God with thankful hearts.

Colossians 3:16 NLT

Your word is a lamp for my feet
and a light for my path.

Psalm 119:105 GW

But Jesus answered, "Rather, how happy are those who hear the word of God and obey it!"

Luke 11:28 GNT

If you remain in me and my words remain in you, ask whatever you wish, and it will be done for you.

John 15:7 NIV

STRENGTHS AND GIFTS

Dear Lord,

Who am I and what do I have that is of any value if I don't have You or the gifts You've given me? For, though the wages You paid for sin was death, the gift You've given to me is eternal life through Jesus Christ my Lord.

It is by Your grace that I have been saved by faith. I did nothing to earn my salvation by my own efforts. It was a gift of love from You, brought to me by the work of Christ Jesus on the cross.

And to make this gift even better, You have given me the very presence of Your Holy Spirit to work inside of me.

Now that I have Your Spirit within me, I do not need to live in fear, for Your Spirit fills me with power, love, and self-control and gives me a sound mind.

For You are my source and supply. You give me strength and power when I feel weak.

You anoint me with the ability to do all things through the strength of Christ.

How joyful I feel that I have Your grace as well as Your might.

Thank You, Lord.

For the wages of sin is death, but the gift of God is eternal life in Christ Jesus our Lord.

Romans 6:23 NIV

For it is by God's grace that you have been saved through faith. It is not the result of your own efforts, but God's gift, so that no one can boast about it.

Ephesians 2:8 GNT

For the Spirit that God has given us does not make us timid; instead, his Spirit fills us with power, love, and self-control.

2 Timothy 1:7 GNT

He gives strength to the weak. And He gives power to him who has little strength.

Isaiah 40:29 NLV

I can do all this through him who gives me strength.

Philippians 4:13 NIV

THANKFULNESS

Dear Lord,

Your presence in my life has erased the darkness that once surrounded me. How happy I am to give thanks to You! For You are good, and Your love for me never wavers but endures forever.

As I remember what You rescued me from, I sing to You with joy and shout to You, the Rock of my salvation. As I think of what my life was like before I met You, I burst with thanksgiving and sing songs of praise. For You are great and the King above all gods. The lowly gods of this world cannot compare with Your majesty.

You hold the depths of the earth in Your hands and the snow-capped mountain peaks are Yours. Not only did You make the sea, but You also own it. You formed the land with Your hands.

And You made me too, and made me complete by filling me with Your Spirit. So, I sing psalms and make melody in my heart to You. I joyfully give thanks to You for everything.

Thank You, Lord.

Oh give thanks to the Lord, for he is good;
for his steadfast love endures forever!

1 Chronicles 16:34 ESV

Come, let us sing for joy to the Lord;
let us shout aloud to the Rock of our salvation.
Let us come before him with thanksgiving
and extol him with music and song.

For the Lord is the great God,
the great King above all gods.
In his hand are the depths of the earth,
and the mountain peaks belong to him.
The sea is his, for he made it,
and his hands formed the dry land.

Psalm 95:1–5 NIV

But be filled with the Spirit, speaking to one another in psalms and hymns and spiritual songs, singing and making melody with your hearts to the Lord; always giving thanks for all things in the name of our Lord Jesus Christ to our God and Father.

Ephesians 5:18–20 NASB

TRIUMPH

Dear Lord,

Drums beat, horses gallop, and war cries rise as approaching warriors wave their swords, ready for battle. Though I'm impressed by the strength of my enemy, I will not retreat.

When I think of the fight ahead, how thankful I am that You, my Lord, are going into it before me, with me, and through me. The enemy cannot defeat me when You are at my side. The reason is simple: even when I am weak, You are strong, and no one can defeat You. The enemy can only flee before You as You hand me the win.

How humble I am that You have already granted the desires of my heart, turning my battles into victories. I shout for joy over every triumph. I lift my banner in the honor of my God.

Lord, the reason You grant all my requests is because You have anointed me for success.

You answer me from Your heavenly sanctuary with the victorious power of Your right hand.

Because I've been born again through the power of Jesus, I am a new creature in Christ. That's how I gain victory over the world. What joy that my faith ensures triumph over my foes through the power of my Lord Jesus Christ.

Thank You, Lord.

The LORD your God is going with you. He will fight for you against your enemies and give you victory.

Deuteronomy 20:4 GW

May he give you the desire of your heart
and make all your plans succeed.
May we shout for joy over your victory
and lift up our banners in the name of our God.

May the LORD grant all your requests.

Now this I know:
The LORD gives victory to his anointed.
He answers him from his heavenly sanctuary
with the victorious power of his right hand.

Psalm 20:4–6 NIV

Because everyone who has been born from God has won the victory over the world. Our faith is what wins the victory over the world.

1 John 5:4 GW

But thanks be to God! He gives us the victory through our Lord Jesus Christ.

1 Corinthians 15:57 NIV

DEFEATING *joy* STEALERS

Guard your heart more than anything else,
because the source of your life flows from it.

Proverbs 4:23 GW

Because no matter how vigorously you try to justify the disobedience in your life, you can never replace the joy that is lost when you say no to God.

Dr. David Jeremiah

ANGER

Dear Lord,

Red-hot anger burns my cheeks. If only I could push back, treat those who hurt me the way they treated me. If only I could tell them what I really think, I would feel so righteous. But the problem with this kind of "righteousness" is that it's self-indulgent and it's not of You. Instead, You want me to do what? Bless them? Isn't that the opposite of what they deserve?

Maybe, but You ask me not to pay back evil with evil but to pay back evil with blessings because You are blessing me.

Okay, I'm counting to ten and focusing on You. I will bless my enemies by praying that Your love will open blind eyes so that those who hurt me can experience Your love, so they can be blessed as You have blessed me. I will do it Your way and respond to those who oppose me with kindness and forgiveness because Christ has forgiven me.

It's hard to open my heart like this, but as it turns out, the source of my life flows from my heart. I know this flow is from the Holy Spirit who is producing rivers of love, joy, peace, and more. The bonus is that these attitudes of humble forgiveness are never wrong in Your eyes.

You remind me that it's easier for me to take a city with Holy Spirit–inspired self-control than it is for me to set my face to war. Besides, where's the joy in fighting? Therefore, I turn my face to You and respond with Your love to those who mistreat me.

Thank You, Lord.

Do not pay back evil with evil or cursing with cursing; instead, pay back with a blessing, because a blessing is what God promised to give you when he called you.

1 Peter 3:9 GNT

Get rid of all bitterness, rage, anger, harsh words, and slander, as well as all types of evil behavior. Instead, be kind to each other, tenderhearted, forgiving one another, just as God through Christ has forgiven you.

Ephesians 4:31–32 NLT

Guard your heart more than anything else,
because the source of your life flows from it.

Proverbs 4:23 GW

But the Holy Spirit produces this kind of fruit in our lives: love, joy, peace, patience, kindness, goodness, faithfulness, gentleness, and self-control. There is no law against these things!

Galatians 5:22–23 NLT

Better a patient person than a warrior,
one with self-control than one who takes a city.

Proverbs 16:32 NIV

ANXIETY

Dear Lord,

Because I'm seeking more joy in my life, I've realized the first step I must take is to ask You to examine my heart. As You do, please help me stop my worries and anxious thoughts from tumbling in an endless spin cycle.

Endlessly spinning my worries is not Your ideal for me. I confess my anxious thoughts and invite You to be the solution to every one of them. Comfort me and remind me that You have a plan to turn my worries into blessings. That plan is already in progress and happens whenever I trust in You.

As I decide to trust You, my troubled heart changes into a heart filled with peace. That peace grows when I realize Your perfect One is in me.

Therefore, when I'm afraid, I will put my trust in You.

As I'm trusting You, I will no longer be anxious about anything. And when worries arise, I will pray about them and ask for Your solutions. I will pray about all my stress points, which is exactly what You called me to do. You want me to tell You about my needs as I give my requests to You. But my focus should be thankfulness for all Your blessings. What joy that You care for me and that I can turn over my anxieties to You.

Thank You, Lord.

Examine me, God! Look at my heart!
Put me to the test! Know my anxious thoughts!

Psalm 139:23 CEB

When my anxieties multiply,
your comforting calms me down.

Psalm 94:19 CEB

Do not let your hearts be troubled. You believe in God; believe also in me.

John 14:1 NIV

But when I am afraid,
I will put my trust in you.

Psalm 56:3 NLT

Don't be anxious about things; instead, pray. Pray about everything. He longs to hear your requests, so talk to God about your needs and be thankful for what has come.

Philippians 4:6 VOICE

Turn all your anxiety over to God because he cares for you.

1 Peter 5:7 GW

BITTERNESS

Dear Lord,

Just as a small fire can be squelched with a wet blanket, love can squelch wrongs and even prevent the flame of quarrels. Even so, I find that it's hard to be at peace with everyone in my life. But how can I shine Your love if I respond to wrongs with hate?

Help me guard myself against withholding Your grace, for when I do, I look like a bad case of poison ivy, a person itching to cause trouble.

Even worse, my bitter thoughts act like arsenic to my own relationship with You. The antidote to this kind of poison is to apply Your compassionate kindness, a kindness that allows me to graciously forgive, just as You have forgiven me through Jesus, who liberated me from my sin.

So, I bow my head and pray for those who are my enemies and all those who persecute me. Help them to see You, Lord, as You clothe me in Your peace. Help me to forgive them as I let go of my own grudges and hold on to my joy.

Your words show me that You count my bitterness as sin. So, even though I've been wronged, I let go of my bitterness and lay this poison at Your feet so it will no longer course through my heart. I extend my gratitude to You, my dear Lord, knowing that You forgive me too.

Thank You, Lord.

Hate starts quarrels,
but love covers every wrong.

Proverbs 10:12 GW

Try to be at peace with everyone, and try to live a holy life, because no one will see the Lord without it. Guard against turning back from the grace of God. Let no one become like a bitter plant that grows up and causes many troubles with its poison.

Hebrews 12:14–15 GNT

Banish bitterness, rage and anger, shouting and slander, and any and all malicious thoughts—these are poison. Instead, be kind and compassionate. Graciously forgive one another just as God has forgiven you through the Anointed, our Liberating King.

Ephesians 4:31–32 VOICE

But I tell you this: Love your enemies, and pray for those who persecute you.

Matthew 5:44 GW

But when you are praying, first forgive anyone you are holding a grudge against, so that your Father in heaven will forgive your sins, too.

Mark 11:25 NLT

COMPARISON

Dear Lord,

Who am I to argue with You, my Creator? I've never heard a clay pot complain or call the potter careless. And since I'm clay in Your hands, I have no reason to grumble as You mold me into the vessel You've planned for my life to become. I'm a one-of-a-kind design that You've created for a purpose, a special function in the body of Christ.

I may wish my assignment included more recognition or appreciation, but the truth is, I belong to the body and the body belongs to me.

What joy that You have given each person in Your body special gifts we can use to serve You and one another. May I serve not with envy but with gladness.

And that's another reason why I praise You, Lord, for Your works are wonderful. I rejoice in knowing that I have been fearfully and wonderfully made.

Just as I shouldn't envy the gifts of others, neither should I boast in my own gifts. For I did not create them; You gave them to me. I can only thank You as I serve You with joy.

You, dear Lord, will finish all that You started in me. Not only does Your faithful love last forever, but You never give up on me or my calling. You give me the wisdom and strength to fulfill all my purposes in You.

Thank You, Lord.

What sorrow awaits those who argue with their Creator.
    Does a clay pot argue with its maker?
Does the clay dispute with the one who shapes it, saying,
    "Stop, you're doing it wrong!"
Does the pot exclaim,
    "How clumsy can you be?"

Isaiah 45:9 NLT

Just as our bodies have many parts and each part has a special function, so it is with Christ's body. We are many parts of one body, and we all belong to each other.

In his grace, God has given us different gifts for doing certain things well.

Romans 12:4–6 NLT

I praise you because I am fearfully and wonderfully made;
    your works are wonderful,
    I know that full well.

Psalm 139:14 NIV

Who made you superior to others? Didn't God give you everything you have? Well, then, how can you boast, as if what you have were not a gift?

1 Corinthians 4:7 GNT

The Eternal will finish what He started in me.
    Your faithful love, O Eternal One, lasts forever;
    do not give up on what Your hands have made.

Psalm 138:8 VOICE

CONFUSION

Dear Lord,

With so many different spirits and spiritual practices around, I must not be tricked into following a spirit that claims it is from You when it isn't.

Your Word says I can recognize truth when a person, religious organization, or spirit declares that Jesus has come from You.

If a spirit claims that You cannot identify Jesus as Your Son, I'm most likely dealing with a spirit who hates Christ.

This is a good test to know so I can avoid falling into confusion.

For with joy, I agree with this truth: I know that You are my God. There is no confusion, strife, or hate in You. You are the author of love and peace.

So I will joyfully declare Jesus as the only way to You, the real Truth and Life who said, "No one comes to the Father but through me."

How joyful to know that when I believe this, repent of my sins, and follow Jesus, I will receive Your presence in my life—the Spirit of truth!

With joy, I repent now, I turn now, I follow Jesus now. I receive the Spirit of truth, Your holy presence, in my life now.

Lord, thank You that I will hear Your voice and be guided by Your Spirit. Keep me close so I can follow You all the days of my life.

Thank You, Lord.

My dear friends, do not believe all who claim to have the Spirit, but test them to find out if the spirit they have comes from God. For many false prophets have gone out everywhere. This is how you will be able to know whether it is God's Spirit: anyone who acknowledges that Jesus Christ came as a human being has the Spirit who comes from God. But anyone who denies this about Jesus does not have the Spirit from God. The spirit that he has is from the Enemy of Christ; you heard that it would come, and now it is here in the world already.

1 John 4:1–3 GNT

For God is not the author of confusion but of peace, as in all the churches of the saints.

1 Corinthians 14:33 NKJV

Jesus said to him, "I am the [only] Way [to God] and the [real] Truth and the [real] Life; no one comes to the Father but through Me.

John 14:6 AMP

When the Spirit of Truth comes, he will guide you into the full truth. He won't speak on his own. He will speak what he hears and will tell you about things to come.

John 16:13 GW

DARKNESS

Dear Lord,

I was once bumping into walls and stumbling in the dark, but now I'm living in the light of Your love. No longer is my life filled with darkness, because You shone the light from the beautiful face of Jesus straight into my heart. This gift has forever rescued me from eternal darkness.

When I finally understood that Jesus is Your Son, it was like You turned on a light so I would no longer fall into traps. Suddenly everything became bright and clear. My darkness disappeared, and I could clearly see how to walk with You.

For Jesus proclaimed that He is the light sent from You when He said, "I am the light of the world. He who follows Me shall not walk in darkness, but have the light of life."

Jesus is my joy, the source of my life. He shines through the darkness, and the darkness can never extinguish His light.

Thank You, Lord.

At one time you lived in darkness. Now you are living in the light that comes from the Lord. Live as children who have the light of the Lord in them.

Ephesians 5:8 NLV

The God who said, "Out of darkness the light shall shine!" is the same God who made his light shine in our hearts, to bring us the knowledge of God's glory shining in the face of Christ.

2 Corinthians 4:6 GNT

You are the lamp who lights my way;
the Eternal, my God, lights up my darkness.

Psalm 18:28 VOICE

Then Jesus spoke to them again, saying, "I am the light of the world. He who follows Me shall not walk in darkness, but have the light of life."

John 8:12 NKJV

The Light shines in the darkness. The darkness has never been able to put out the Light.

John 1:5 NLV

DEPRESSION

Dear Lord,

When the music stops, the world weeps, and my life fills with sadness, You remind me to pray, so I'm praying to You right now.

Help me, Lord.

No matter my emotional state, You remind me to be strong and courageous and to live without fear. This instruction marks the way out of despair, a way I will follow one step, one day at a time.

How blessed I am at the news that You have promised to be with me whether I'm in a state of happiness or working my way out of a state of depression.

Not only do You bandage my wounds, You have the power to heal my broken heart, and I ask that You heal my heart now.

In fact, I run into Your arms, exhausted by the battles raging in my life, exhausted by the heavy burdens I've carried. As I quiet my soul in You, I begin to realize Your love for me. I finally get the presence of mind to exchange my wounds, as well as the weight of my burdens, for Your peace that passes understanding.

This is another great reason to stick with You and ask You to restore my joy.

So yes, I receive Your joy and ask You to help me realize the blessings that are already mine. Help me to approach You with gratitude so I can live a joyful life in You.

Thank You, Lord.

Are any of you suffering hardships? You should pray. Are any of you happy? You should sing praises.

James 5:13 NLT

Have I not commanded you? Be strong and courageous. Do not be afraid; do not be discouraged, for the LORD your God will be with you wherever you go.

Joshua 1:9 NIV

He is the healer of the brokenhearted.
He is the one who bandages their wounds.

Psalm 147:3 GW

Come to me, all you who are weary and burdened, and I will give you rest.

Matthew 11:28 NIV

I have told you this so that you will have peace by being united to me. The world will make you suffer. But be brave! I have defeated the world!

John 16:33 GNT

DISAPPOINTMENTS OF THE PAST

Dear Lord,

In times of trouble, I hide in You and I'm safe.

When I call to You, not only do You hear me, You listen and rescue me from my difficulties. When I'm discouraged, You are near. When I have lost all hope, You save me.

That is why I can rejoice when I run into problems and trials. That is because my trials help me develop endurance, and endurance helps me develop strength of character, which in turn strengthens my hope of salvation. This hope never leads to disappointments because I know You love me dearly. I know this is true because You have given me Your Holy Spirit to fill my heart with Your love.

Because I believe in You, I will not be disappointed. I have Your power to help restore my joyful heart. I trusted that I would see Your goodness while still living on this earth, and I have.

Even in disappointments and difficulties, I will wait on You with courage. You strengthen my heart, and I rejoice in You.

Thank You, Lord.

The Lord is good, a safe place in times of trouble. And He knows those who come to Him to be safe.

Nahum 1:7 NLV

We can rejoice, too, when we run into problems and trials, for we know that they help us develop endurance. And endurance develops strength of character, and character strengthens our confident hope of salvation. And this hope will not lead to disappointment. For we know how dearly God loves us, because he has given us the Holy Spirit to fill our hearts with his love.

Romans 5:3–5 NLT

We are often troubled, but not crushed; sometimes in doubt, but never in despair; there are many enemies, but we are never without a friend; and though badly hurt at times, we are not destroyed.

2 Corinthians 4:8–9 GNT

The scripture says, "Whoever believes in him will not be disappointed."

Romans 10:11 GNT

I would have lost heart, unless I had believed
That I would see the goodness of the Lord
In the land of the living.

Wait on the Lord;
Be of good courage,
And He shall strengthen your heart;
Wait, I say, on the Lord!

Psalm 27:13–14 NKJV

DISCOURAGEMENT

Dear Lord,

When Your servant Job faced one calamity after the other, his friends gathered around him, not to comfort him but to mock him and accuse him of sinning against You. But Job maintained his innocence and responded, "Though he slay me, yet will I hope in him."

Job's words inspire me in my times of discouragement. If Job could trust You, even in the face of loss, mockery, and death, then I can trust You, even in the face of my own calamities.

The psalmist David also faced discouragement as he lived on the run, dodging the armies of his own father-in-law. King Saul would have killed David if he could have caught him, but You protected David from capture. David rejoiced in You because when he sought You, You answered him and delivered him from his fears. That's one of the reasons David declared that all who look to You are radiant, their faces unashamed.

Let my countenance also shine as I praise You.

Just as You did with David, You hear my cries and pay attention to my prayers!

When my heart is weak, I call to You. Lead me to safety, to Your rock of refuge, a tower of strength in the face of my enemies. Let me live in Your tent forever, and keep me under the shelter of Your wings.

I will always pour out my heart to You, for You are my safe place and I trust You.

Thank You, Lord.

Though he slay me, yet will I hope in him.

Job 13:15 NIV

I sought the Lord, and he answered me;
he delivered me from all my fears.
Those who look to him are radiant;
their faces are never covered with shame.

Psalm 34:4–5 NIV

God, listen to my cry;
pay attention to my prayer!
When my heart is weak,
I cry out to you from the very ends of the earth.
Lead me to the rock that is higher than I am
because you have been my refuge,
a tower of strength in the face of the enemy.
Please let me live in your tent forever!
Please let me take refuge
in the shelter of your wings! *Selah*

Psalm 61:1–4 CEB

Trust in Him at all times, O people. Pour out your heart before Him. God is a safe place for us.

Psalm 62:8 NLV

FATIGUE

Dear Lord,

When my spirit is broken, I feel worn out. But when I have a joyful heart, it's like medicine to my body.

Sometimes it's hard to wait on You, but when I do, You give me new strength. You give me the power to rise with wings like eagles. You enable me to run and not grow tired. In Your power, I can walk and not feel weak.

That is why I'm determined to wait on You, to always follow You. For when I seek after Your face, I always find the strength I need for my journey.

Lord, You are better than a strong cup of coffee because You energize me with Your presence. You are my strength and my song! You are my Savior and my God, and I will praise You, the God of my fathers. I will give all honor to You.

I ask that you supernaturally strengthen me as I live my life empowered through my union with You, my Lord Jesus. Because of You, I will stand victorious in the power of Your boundless might.

Thank You, Lord.

A cheerful heart is good medicine,
but a broken spirit saps a person's strength.

Proverbs 17:22 NLT

But they who wait upon the Lord will get new strength. They will rise up with wings like eagles. They will run and not get tired. They will walk and not become weak.

Isaiah 40:31 NLV

Always follow the Eternal,
His strength and His face.

1 Chronicles 16:11 VOICE

The LORD is my strength and my song.
He is my Savior.
This is my God, and I will praise him,
my father's God, and I will honor him.

Exodus 15:2 GW

In conclusion, be strong in the Lord [draw your strength from Him and be empowered through your union with Him] and in the power of His [boundless] might.

Ephesians 6:10 AMP

FEAR

Dear Lord,

Your Spirit fills my heart with power, love, and a sound mind so that there is no room for fear.

Therefore, I don't entertain anxious thoughts, which try to pull me in the direction of dread. I sidestep this fear trap by turning to You in prayer, talking to You about my needs, with gratitude, knowing that You long to hear my requests. How thankful I feel as You fill my heart with peace. A peace that gives me joy, knowing it is a gift beyond my understanding, a gift that guards my heart and mind through Jesus Christ.

You have told me not to be afraid or allow intimidation to control me because You are with me. You are my God. You promised to strengthen me, to help me, to support me with Your right hand of victory.

When fear walks into my life, I rush to lay it at Your feet. Releasing my fear to You enables me to trust You with my whole heart. Besides, with the Lord of the universe at my side, who can harm me? I will not be afraid of what is to come.

My heart rejoices with praise as I trust in Your promises.

Thank You, Lord.

For God has not given us a spirit of fear, but of power and of love and of a sound mind.

2 Timothy 1:7 NKJV

Don't be anxious about things; instead, pray. Pray about everything. He longs to hear your requests, so talk to God about your needs and be thankful for what has come. And know that the peace of God (a peace that is beyond any and all of our human understanding) will stand watch over your hearts and minds in Jesus, the Anointed One.

Philippians 4:6–7 VOICE

Don't be afraid, because I am with you.
Don't be intimidated; I am your God.
I will strengthen you.
I will help you.
I will support you with my victorious right hand.

Isaiah 41:10 GW

When I am afraid, O Lord Almighty,
I put my trust in you.
I trust in God and am not afraid;
I praise him for what he has promised.
What can a mere human being do to me?

Psalm 56:3–4 GNT

NEGATIVE THOUGHTS

Dear Lord,

I've had a lot of bosses in my life, but the worst boss I've ever had is me. I let myself get away with sinful thoughts and deeds. But since the wages of sin is death, this setup makes for a terrifying payday, with a paycheck I'd rather skip. But when I give myself to You and ask You to be the boss of my life, Your presence rests on me. Your Holy Spirit rules my mind and helps me to make better choices. I'm able to exchange my old wages of death for life and peace.

This is exactly why I shouldn't copy worldly customs and dwell on sin, envy, strife, and bitterness. These kinds of thoughts poison my heart. But when I allow the presence of the Holy Spirit to change the way I think, my eyes pop open and I can see Your pleasing and perfect will.

Therefore, I put myself under Your authority, reject my old mindsets, and resist the devil. When he sees the new me, he's terrified and backs off.

Lord, I will guard my heart because the source of my life flows through what I've tucked inside of it. I will cast off negative thoughts and concentrate on what is true, noble, right, pure, lovely, admirable, and praiseworthy.

As I do, my thoughts turn to peace, and I find joy in belonging to You.

Thank You, Lord.

If your sinful old self is the boss over your mind, it leads to death. But if the Holy Spirit is the boss over your mind, it leads to life and peace.

Romans 8:6 NLV

Don't copy the behavior and customs of this world, but let God transform you into a new person by changing the way you think. Then you will learn to know God's will for you, which is good and pleasing and perfect.

Romans 12:2 NLT

So place yourselves under God's authority. Resist the devil, and he will run away from you.

James 4:7 GW

Guard your heart more than anything else,
because the source of your life flows from it.

Proverbs 4:23 GW

Finally, brothers and sisters, whatever is true, whatever is noble, whatever is right, whatever is pure, whatever is lovely, whatever is admirable—if anything is excellent or praiseworthy—think about such things.

Philippians 4:8 NIV

PAIN

Dear Lord,

I once heard that You want me to be joyful in my trials. Pardon me, but that sounds backwards; shouldn't joy be reserved for my happiest of times?

I thought so, until I found myself in the middle of trouble. To my surprise, trouble was the place where my faith produced patience, and patience worked to make me more complete in You. It wasn't that I enjoyed the pain, but You gave me joy through my pain.

The things I'm suffering now are barely worth mentioning because they can't be compared with Your glory to come.

In that day, You will wipe away my tears. There will be no more death or pandemics, grief, crying, or even pain. Those things will be over.

But for now, I shelter in You as I hide in Your shadow. I declare that You are my refuge and my fortress, my God in whom I trust.

You rescue me from traps set by the enemy and make me safe from deadly plagues.

Even when I'm in hot water up to my neck, You are with me. I will not be swept away by rivers of trouble, and I will walk through the fire and not be destroyed or even burned.

Thank You, Lord.

My brethren, count it all joy when you fall into various trials, knowing that the testing of your faith produces patience. But let patience have its perfect work, that you may be perfect and complete, lacking nothing.

James 1:2–4 NKJV

For I consider that the sufferings of this present time are not worthy to be compared with the glory which shall be revealed in us.

Romans 8:18 NKJV

He will wipe every tear from their eyes. There won't be any more death. There won't be any grief, crying, or pain, because the first things have disappeared.

Revelation 21:4 GW

Whoever lives under the shelter of the Most High
will remain in the shadow of the Almighty.
I will say to the Lord,
"You are my refuge and my fortress, my God in whom I trust."

He is the one who will rescue you from hunters' traps
and from deadly plagues.

Psalm 91:1–3 GW

When you pass through the waters, I will be with you. When you pass through the rivers, they will not flow over you. When you walk through the fire, you will not be burned. The fire will not destroy you.

Isaiah 43:2 NLV

STRESS

Dear Lord,

When my worries drove me crazy, Your comfort brought joy to my soul. When I finally got tired of trying to figure out my problems by myself, I called to You and not only did You answer me, You set me free. Your protection helped me realize that there's no need to fear. Who can hurt me with You around?

I've discovered that worry is never productive. Why should I give worry power over my life when worry can't even add a single hour to it?

I need to drop my relationship with worry and exchange it for what produces the most peace and joy in my life: putting my trust in You. I need to stop fretting and relying on my own perceptions, which are not the same as Your better vantage point. I only need to look to Your guidance, and You will handle my problems in miraculous ways.

Lord, help me to keep my faith strong, even when I'm surrounded by troubles. When I learn to trust You, Your blessings arrive just when I need them.

How happy I am when I pass the trials and tests of life. My reward will come the day You call me home. You will smile at me with approval and give me the victorious crown of life. You promised this victory crown because I love You.

Thank You, Lord.

When my worry is great within me, Your comfort brings
joy to my soul.

Psalm 94:19 NLV

In my distress I called to the LORD;
he answered me and set me free.
The LORD is with me, I will not be afraid;
what can anyone do to me?

Psalm 118:5–6 GNT

Can any of you add a single hour to your life by worrying?

Matthew 6:27 GW

Trust in the LORD with all your heart. Never rely on what you think you know. Remember the LORD in everything you do, and he will show you the right way.

Proverbs 3:5–6 GNT

Happy is the person who can hold up under the trials of life. At the right time, he'll know God's sweet approval and will be crowned with life. As God has promised, the crown awaits all who love Him.

James 1:12 VOICE

TROUBLE

Dear Lord,

Why do I let my heart be troubled when I have peace in You? Your presence in my life is why I do not need to run away from tests or hardships. You have shown me that trusting You through trials is my secret path to peace and joy. Trials build endurance and give me the strength I need to cross my finish line mature, complete, and wanting nothing.

Trusting You in trouble is a choice I face daily. I can choose to be afraid, or I can choose to be strong and courageous so that I have confidence to face whoever comes against me.

For my trust is in You, my God; You are the One who stands up for me and never leaves or abandons me.

You are my refuge when I'm oppressed, a safe place in times of trouble.

I trust You because I know You, and from my experiences, I know You will never turn away from me.

I've learned these lessons because there was a time I didn't know You. In those days I was desperate and defeated. But when I cried out to You, You heard me. You saved me from my troubles with a miracle when I needed it most. What joy I have because You are with me in trouble.

Thank You, Lord.

Do not let your hearts be troubled. You believe in God; believe also in me.

John 14:1 NIV

Don't run from tests and hardships, brothers and sisters. As difficult as they are, you will ultimately find joy in them; if you embrace them, your faith will blossom under pressure and teach you true patience as you endure. And true patience brought on by endurance will equip you to complete the long journey and cross the finish line—mature, complete, and wanting nothing.

James 1:2–4 VOICE

Be strong and courageous. Do not be afraid or terrified because of them, for the LORD your God goes with you; he will never leave you nor forsake you.

Deuteronomy 31:6 NIV

The LORD is a refuge for the oppressed,
a place of safety in times of trouble.
Those who know you, LORD, will trust you;
you do not abandon anyone who comes to you.

Psalm 9:9–10 GNT

When I had nothing, desperate and defeated,
I cried out to the Lord and he heard me,
bringing his miracle-deliverance when I needed it most.

Psalm 34:6 TPT

UNLOVED

Dear Lord,

How often have I heard the enemy whisper that You could never love me?

What a *lie*!

It's a lie because the thief is a liar. His mission is to steal, kill, and destroy. But the Word reveals that You are truth and that You have come to give me life in all its fullness.

I'm no longer falling for the "God doesn't love me" lie. After all, You, Jesus, are the Good Shepherd, and You loved me so much that You died for me so that I could have abundant life in You.

The fact is that seven hundred years before You were born of a virgin in Bethlehem, the prophet Isaiah wrote of You, saying the Spirit of the Lord would be on You to bring good news to the poor, to heal those with sad hearts, and to free those who were held prisoner.

I'm one of the people You came to set free. You came for me because You love me!

Because I'm in awe of You, Your loving-kindness is forever on me. You don't just love me, You love my family. Your Word says You will bless me as well as my children and grandchildren.

I have experienced a deeper love encounter with You and am learning to trust in the love You have for me. For I live in You and Your love, and You live in me.

Thank You for Your love, for Your love gives me joy.

Thank You, Lord.

The thief comes only in order to steal, kill, and destroy. I have come in order that you might have life—life in all its fullness.
I am the good shepherd, who is willing to die for the sheep.

John 10:10–11 GNT

The Spirit of the Lord God is on me, because the Lord has chosen me to bring good news to poor people. He has sent me to heal those with a sad heart. He has sent me to tell those who are being held and those in prison that they can go free.

Isaiah 61:1 NLV

But the loving-kindness of the Lord is forever and forever on those who fear Him. And what is right with God is given forever to their children's children, to those who keep His agreement and remember to obey His Law.

Psalm 103:17–18 NLV

We have come to know [by personal observation and experience], and have believed [with deep, consistent faith] the love which God has for us. God is love, and the one who abides in love abides in God, and God abides continually in him.

1 John 4:16 AMP

WORRY

Dear Lord,

You want me to stop worrying about tomorrow and deal with the challenges of today without adding my worries to my troubles. You even promise that tomorrow's challenges will take care of themselves.

You remind me that the only way to accomplish this worry-free attitude is through prayer.

Your prayer instructions say I'm to let You know everything I need and even to say "Thank You, Lord!" before You answer.

Help me follow these instructions daily, because this is the secret to peace that is beyond anything I can imagine. Praying this way will guard my thoughts and emotions through Christ Jesus.

Not only do You remind me that You care for me, You invite me to hand off my burdens and worries to You. What a freeing idea!

So I ask You now, please carry my burdens and worries so I can be free to enjoy more of Your presence in my life.

Jesus, Your invitation to give You my heavy burdens comes with the wonderful promise that You will exchange my burdens for Your rest. For Your yoke is easy to bear and Your burden is light.

Not only do You make my steps lighter, but You also richly fill my needs.

How glorious! How wonderful that You are so good to me! What a joy it is to serve You!

Thank You, Lord.

So do not worry about tomorrow; it will have enough worries of its own. There is no need to add to the troubles each day brings.

Matthew 6:34 GNT

Never worry about anything. But in every situation let God know what you need in prayers and requests while giving thanks. Then God's peace, which goes beyond anything we can imagine, will guard your thoughts and emotions through Christ Jesus.

Philippians 4:6–7 GW

Since God cares for you, let Him carry all your burdens and worries.

1 Peter 5:7 VOICE

Then Jesus said, "Come to me, all of you who are weary and carry heavy burdens, and I will give you rest. Take my yoke upon you. Let me teach you, because I am humble and gentle at heart, and you will find rest for your souls. For my yoke is easy to bear, and the burden I give you is light."

Matthew 11:28–30 NLT

My God will richly fill your every need in a glorious way through Christ Jesus.

Philippians 4:19 GW

RECLAIMING

May God, the source of hope, fill you with joy and peace through your faith in him. Then you will overflow with hope by the power of the Holy Spirit.

Romans 15:13 GW

The things we try to avoid and fight against—tribulation, suffering, and persecution—are the very things that produce abundant joy in us. "We are more than conquerors through Him" "in all these things"; not in spite of them, but in the midst of them.

Oswald Chambers

BLESSED

Dear Lord,

It would be so wonderful if my life came with perfect circumstances, perfect health, and a shiny, sin-free soul. But I'm far from perfect, which means my sin prevents me from walking with You, a holy God. But You, Lord, made a way so that we could walk together and share a deep friendship. Not only have You covered my sins through the blood of Jesus, but You are also with me and never leave my side. You bless me, even in my difficulties; You turn my struggles into blessings.

You use struggles to chisel me into Your image. My problems prompt me to call and rely on You. You give me deeper communion with You as I learn to seek and trust You through my earthly journey. Leaning into Your faithfulness produces such a blessing of joy.

Help me to endure the tests You allow as I continue to love You all the days of my life. How I look forward to the day I wear Your crown of life.

Problems are mere stepping-stones in my path of joy, for You are always good.

You are the One who blesses and protects me. You are the One who smiles on me as You bless me. You are the One who gives me favor and peace. Thank You, Lord; I receive Your blessings.

Your blessings overwhelm me more than I could ever imagine. Thank You that You take care of me in every way. Remind me to share my blessings with others so I can experience even more of Your joy.

Thank You, Lord.

My beloved friend, I pray that everything is going well for you and that your body is as healthy as your soul is prosperous.

3 John 1:2 VOICE

Blessed are those who endure when they are tested. When they pass the test, they will receive the crown of life that God has promised to those who love him.

James 1:12 GW

Oh, taste and see that the LORD is good;
Blessed is the man who trusts in Him!

Psalm 34:8 NKJV

May the LORD bless you
and protect you.
May the LORD smile on you
and be gracious to you.
May the LORD show you his favor
and give you his peace.

Numbers 6:24–26 NLT

God is ready to overwhelm you with more blessings than you could ever imagine so that you'll always be taken care of in every way and you'll have more than enough to share.

2 Corinthians 9:8 VOICE

BREAKING FREE FROM LIES

Dear Lord,

Set me free from the lies of the enemy. Satan would have me believe that I'm too broken, too ruined by my sin and the sin that's been committed against me, to ever be worthy of Your love. And the truth is, I'm not worthy.

But I must not forget who You are. You are the God of love. When I recognize this truth, it's so much easier to turn my focus from my unworthiness to You and Your love for me. I say yes to Your love and acknowledge that I'm loved by You. My healing, my being able to break free from the enemy's lies, starts with this truth. This truth opens my blind eyes so I can see You.

Because You love me, I want to express my love to You not just through my words but through my actions.

Your Word says that love is patient and kind, never jealous, conceited, or proud. It's never rude, selfish, or irritable, nor does it keep a list of wrongs. Love is never happy about evil but is happy about truth.

There is joy in the truth that You, Lord Jesus, are the Word made flesh. You dwelled among us, coming to us as a gift from the Father, full of grace and truth.

How joyful I am that Your Spirit of truth is in my heart. Your Spirit guides me not into lies but into the truth of who I am in You. Loved and forgiven!

Thank You, Lord.

God is love.

1 John 4:8 NIV

Little children, let us not love in word or talk but in deed and in truth.

1 John 3:18 ESV

Love is patient and kind; it is not jealous or conceited or proud; love is not ill-mannered or selfish or irritable; love does not keep a record of wrongs; love is not happy with evil, but is happy with the truth.

1 Corinthians 13:4–6 GNT

The Word became flesh and made his dwelling among us. We have seen his glory, the glory of the one and only Son, who came from the Father, full of grace and truth.

John 1:14 NIV

When the Spirit of truth comes, he will guide you into all the truth, for he will not speak on his own authority, but whatever he hears he will speak, and he will declare to you the things that are to come.

John 16:13 ESV

BREAKING FREE FROM THE PAST

Dear Lord,

I call out to You from captivity, "Lord, set me free!"

And You hear my cry and send me Your answer—*freedom*!

Now I'm no longer a slave in bondage to sin, fear, or even my past because You, Jesus, rescued me from these chains of death. You set me free, and I am free indeed.

My freedom is a gift that will always belong to me through Christ. I will not follow the enemy into bondage ever again. I will never trade my precious gift of freedom for slavery.

How did You, my God, manage to set me free? You did so by filling my heart with Your Holy Spirit. Fill me so full of You that I'm blind to the enemy's lures and deaf to his call. And I declare the enemy has no claim on me because I belong to You, my precious Lord and Savior.

And now that this freedom is mine, I will live into joy as I give myself to serve You, Lord, by serving others. How wonderful that I can do this through Your marvelous gift of freedom, freedom who has a name—Jesus Christ. I will follow Him forever.

Thank You, Lord.

In my distress I called to the Lord;
he answered me and set me free.

Psalm 118:5 GNT

So if the Son sets you free, you will be free indeed.

John 8:36 NIV

Freedom is what we have—Christ has set us free! Stand, then, as free people, and do not allow yourselves to become slaves again.

Galatians 5:1 GNT

The heart is free where the Spirit of the Lord is. The Lord is the Spirit.

2 Corinthians 3:17 NLV

For you were called to freedom, brothers. Only do not use your freedom as an opportunity for the flesh, but through love serve one another.

Galatians 5:13 ESV

CASTING YOUR CARES

Dear Lord,

The enemy came into this world with the malicious intent to steal, kill, and destroy, but You, Jesus, came to give abundant life. I want to keep my focus on Your abundant life. Why give the enemy more power than he deserves by focusing on him and his dirty tricks? I have more peace when I keep my eyes on You. Looking to You helps me exchange fear and worry for Your joy.

When I take my eyes off You, I let fear control my life.

You promise that I don't need to worry about anything: what I will eat, drink, or wear. You taught that my life is more than my next hot meal, and my body is more than the clothes I wear.

When I watch the birds soar in the sky, I remember that You said birds don't plant, harvest, or gather their crops into barns, which means they do nothing to earn a living. Yet, as You taught, You feed them. You provide all my needs too because You see me as even more valuable than the birds.

Why do I waste my time worrying when I could spend my time thinking about Your provisions for me, the abundant life You've given me? Returning my thoughts to You would certainly replace my fear with joy.

Therefore, Lord, I announce that my worries are now Your problem. I turn my worries over to You because You care about me and will meet my needs with Your blessings.

Thank You, Lord.

The thief approaches with malicious intent, looking to steal, slaughter, and destroy; I came to give life with joy and abundance.

John 10:10 VOICE

So I tell you to stop worrying about what you will eat, drink, or wear. Isn't life more than food and the body more than clothes?

Look at the birds. They don't plant, harvest, or gather the harvest into barns. Yet, your heavenly Father feeds them. Aren't you worth more than they?

Matthew 6:25–26 GW

Turn all your anxiety over to God because he cares for you.

1 Peter 5:7 GW

FORGIVING OTHERS

Dear Lord,

As You know, I'm dealing with a hurt that's most unfair. And the thing is, even though I'm not the one in the wrong, I'm the one who's suffering. It's not right. My bitter feelings are certainly justifiable. Still, I've noticed it's hard to have joy when I'm filled with bitterness.

It seems unreasonable to forgive everyone for everything they've done to hurt me, until I remember that the cost of Your forgiveness for me was the death of Christ on the cross.

I realize that Your command that I forgive others is a small thing when I consider how You had to suffer to forgive me.

When someone hurts me, You want me to be understanding. You want me to forgive because You've forgiven me.

I want to follow Your instruction to forgive those who wrong me. First, I'm to go to them and explain how they hurt me. If they apologize, I'm to forgive them. If they continue to wrong me yet continue to repent, I'm to continue to forgive, even when I must step back to protect myself and others from harm. I can prayerfully share truth in love to help stop dangerous abuse.

As I pray for Your kingdom to come and Your will to be done, You want me to forgive the debts of others even when their debt is failure to repent or apologize. Please give me Your power to lay those who wrong me at Your feet. Otherwise, these people who wrong me become a barrier between us.

Give me Your power to forgive those who hurt me. I trade my bitter heart for a heart of joy. You have set me free!

Thank You, Lord.

You must be kind to each other. Think of the other person. Forgive other people just as God forgave you because of Christ's death on the cross.

Ephesians 4:32 NLV

Try to understand other people. Forgive each other. If you have something against someone, forgive him. That is the way the Lord forgave you.

Colossians 3:13 NLV

So watch yourselves.

If your brother or sister sins against you, rebuke them; and if they repent, forgive them. Even if they sin against you seven times in a day and seven times come back to you saying "I repent," you must forgive them.

Luke 17:3–4 NIV

Instead, we will speak the truth in love, growing in every way more and more like Christ, who is the head of his body, the church.

Ephesians 4:15 NLT

Pray then like this:

"Our Father in heaven,
hallowed be your name.
Your kingdom come,
your will be done,
on earth as it is in heaven.
Give us this day our daily bread,
and forgive us our debts,
as we also have forgiven our debtors.
And lead us not into temptation,
but deliver us from evil."

Matthew 6:9–13 ESV

HEALING HEARTACHE

Dear Lord,

It's hard to smile when my heart aches, when I feel the pain of loss, the sting of disappointment, the wrong of injustice, or the suffering of depression.

But despite the cause of my pain, You are the One who heals my broken heart and bandages my wounds.

When I cry to You for help, You hear me and deliver me from my troubles. You move even closer to me when I'm in emotional pain. You save me when my spirit is crushed.

Trouble may come at me from every direction, but You will deliver me from all of it.

When I look at my life from Your perspective, I see that my life continues past death and into eternity. In that heavenly day You call me home, You will wipe away my every tear. There will be no more loss, death, grief, crying, or pain. All those things will have disappeared into the joy of Your overwhelming love.

But while my life continues here on earth, I need Your comfort. I give You my pain and You give me a glad heart. Help me to keep my focus on Your love and care.

Thank You, Lord.

A glad heart makes a happy face, but when the heart is sad, the spirit is broken.

Proverbs 15:13 NLV

He heals the brokenhearted
and binds up their wounds.

Psalm 147:3 NIV

When the righteous cry for help, the Lord hears
and delivers them out of all their troubles.
The Lord is near to the brokenhearted
and saves the crushed in spirit.

Many are the afflictions of the righteous,
but the Lord delivers him out of them all.
He keeps all his bones;
not one of them is broken.

Psalm 34:17–20 ESV

He will wipe every tear from their eyes. There won't be any more death. There won't be any grief, crying, or pain, because the first things have disappeared.

Revelation 21:4 GW

RENEWED HOPE

Dear Lord,

It's hard to live without hope, but because I belong to You, I do not have to live my life in a state of hopelessness.

Not only will You help me renew my hope, but I can also keep my joy as I hope in You by praising You for every good thing You have put into my life.

Your plans for me are for good, not for evil. Your plans include a future filled with hope.

The reason hope has such power to lift my spirits and satisfy my deepest needs is because Your Holy Spirit has flooded my heart with Your love.

That's why the hope You give me anchors my soul to You in such a sure and steadfast manner. This same hope helps me enter Your hidden presence where You lavish me with joy.

Because I love You, everything that happens to me will work out for my good. This is because You have a wonderful way of using even my difficulties to put me on the path to my destiny.

My joy will arise as I continue to praise You through my hope-filled journey, difficulties and all.

Thank You, Lord.

But as for me, I will always have hope and I will praise You more and more.

Psalm 71:14 NLV

For I know the plans I have for you, declares the LORD, plans for welfare and not for evil, to give you a future and a hope.

Jeremiah 29:11 ESV

And hope will never fail to satisfy our deepest need because the Holy Spirit that was given to us has flooded our hearts with God's love.

Romans 5:5 VOICE

This hope we have as an anchor of the soul, both sure and steadfast, and which enters the Presence behind the veil.

Hebrews 6:19 NKJV

We know that all things work together for the good of those who love God—those whom he has called according to his plan.

Romans 8:28 GW

RENEWING YOUR MIND

Dear Lord,

Create in me a clean heart and renew me with Your love. Reset my thoughts so that I can be free of the cares of this world. But it's not just the world's cares that keep my focus off you; my sins also sidetrack me. This is why I give You permission to renew my mind.

The best way I can partner with You to renew my mind is to read Your Word. Your Word is alive. It guides and convicts me as it keeps me close to You. A renewed mind helps me know what You want me to do. It helps me follow Your plan for me so that my life will be good, pleasing, and perfect.

I will read, think about, and speak Your Word daily, so I can live it. You promise me that when I do, my life will go well and You will give me many good gifts. Renewing my mind strengthens my heart, calms my fears, fortifies my faith, and revitalizes my joy. This kind of focus helps me remember that You are with me wherever I go.

Even as I age, my mind will stay in a perpetual state of renewal, and I will not lose heart.

I will think on things that are true and noble. I will concentrate on things that are fair, just, pure, and lovely. I will meditate on reports about virtuous and praiseworthy things.

This will keep my mind transformed and my heart bursting with joy.

Thank You, Lord.

Create in me a clean heart, O God;
restore within me a sense of being brand new.

Psalm 51:10 VOICE

Do not act like the sinful people of the world. Let God change your life. First of all, let Him give you a new mind. Then you will know what God wants you to do. And the things you do will be good and pleasing and perfect.

Romans 12:2 NLV

Keep this Book of the Law always on your lips; meditate on it day and night, so that you may be careful to do everything written in it. Then you will be prosperous and successful. Have I not commanded you? Be strong and courageous. Do not be afraid; do not be discouraged, for the LORD your God will be with you wherever you go.

Joshua 1:8–9 NIV

So we do not lose heart. Though our outer self is wasting away, our inner self is being renewed day by day.

2 Corinthians 4:16 ESV

Finally, brethren, whatever things are true, whatever things are noble, whatever things are just, whatever things are pure, whatever things are lovely, whatever things are of good report, if there is any virtue and if there is anything praiseworthy—meditate on these things.

Philippians 4:8 NKJV

RESTORING THE JOY OF SALVATION

Dear Lord,

There was a time when I was alive with Your joy as Your Holy Spirit transformed my soul through Your grace and forgiveness. It seems that joy has faded as my soul has grown numb. Maybe I've focused too much on my own pain or the cares of this world, or maybe I've been seduced by sin.

But whatever the cause, I'm on a mission to see my joy restored. So first, I take inventory of my soul and acknowledge my sin. I confess that I have sinned against You and ask that You forgive me and cleanse me from all wrongdoing.

Thank You, Lord, that Jesus took my sin and bore my punishment on the cross. Jesus defeated sin and death when He rose from the dead, creating a way of salvation for me and for all who would follow Him. I receive Your saving power with joy. Strengthen me as I find the willingness to obey You.

Second, I confess I have focused on my own worries as well as the cares of this world instead of keeping my eyes on You. You are the God of hope. Please fill me with Your joy and peace through my faith in You. As my joy and peace increase, You will fill me with hope by the power of Your Spirit.

For joy, peace, and righteousness are not about earthly gain but are blessings brought by the Holy Spirit.

May Your joy be in me so that I overflow with gladness.

Thank You, Lord.

If we confess our sins, he is faithful and just to forgive us our sins and to cleanse us from all unrighteousness.

1 John 1:9 ESV

Let the joy of Your saving power return to me. And give me a willing spirit to obey you.

Psalm 51:12 NLV

May God, the source of hope, fill you with joy and peace through your faith in him. Then you will overflow with hope by the power of the Holy Spirit.

Romans 15:13 GW

For God's Kingdom is not a matter of eating and drinking, but of the righteousness, peace, and joy which the Holy Spirit gives.

Romans 14:17 GNT

I have told you this so that my joy may be in you and that your joy may be complete.

John 15:11 NIV

REVIVING JOY

Dear Lord,

Under Your watch, I've seen hard times and experienced many a miserable day. But instead of blaming You or questioning why a loving God would allow hard things in my life, I determine to look to You with trust. I look to You with a deep knowing that You can use even my difficulties and heartaches in miraculous ways. I call to You in hope, so thankful that You will restore my broken heart as You raise me from the pit of self-pity where I've often found myself.

What I've noticed is that whenever I'm in deep trouble, or feel angry because You allowed that trouble, You never turn Your back on me. Instead, You make me live again, and You send me power to both deflect and defeat the enemy's plans against me. You save and shield me with Your strong hand.

When I feel miserable, You are my comfort. As I open Your Word, the pages revive me. Turn my attention from worthless ponderings and pursuits and wake me to what You've given me, Your tender love and care.

Revive my joy and spare my life with Your kindness. I will recover from my stressors and difficulties as I continue to praise and obey You. As I bless You, my joy shall return.

Thank You, Lord.

You have made me see hard times: I've experienced
many miserable days,
but You will restore me again.
You will raise me up
from the deep pit.

Psalm 71:20 VOICE

Whenever I am in deep trouble,
you make me live again;
you send your power against my enemies' wrath;
you save me with your strong hand.

Psalm 138:7 CEB

This is my comfort in my misery,
That Your word has revived me.

Psalm 119:50 NASB

Turn my eyes away from looking at what is worthless,
And revive me in Your ways.

Psalm 119:37 NASB

Revive me with your tender love and
spare my life by your kindness, and I will continue to
obey you.

Psalm 119:88 TPT

SWEET FELLOWSHIP

Dear Lord,

I don't want to be separated from either You or the body of Christ. Please make a way for me to have continued sweet fellowship with You as well as with other believers.

Break my loneliness by reminding me to be there for others and to carry their burdens.

I know how to care about my own self-interests, but show me how to care about the interests of others. Help me to be motivated not by pride but by humility, thinking of others as better than myself.

I want to live in Your light, and as I do, my fellowship with other believers will continually fill with Your light, because the blood of Jesus continually cleanses me from every sin.

Help me to become aware of others in Your body. For when believers suffer, the whole body of Christ suffers. If believers are praised, the whole body of Christ shares in the joy.

Because I belong to Your body, I'm not a foreigner or an outsider but a fellow citizen, along with all the family of God. Our family was built on the foundation of the apostles and prophets with Jesus Christ as our cornerstone.

In Him, all parts of our building fit together perfectly as we become Your holy temple where Your Spirit dwells. Together, through the power of Christ, we are being filled with Your Holy Spirit so that You may always live in us.

Thank You, Lord.

Help carry each other's burdens. In this way you will follow Christ's teachings.

Galatians 6:2 GW

Don't do anything for selfish purposes, but with humility think of others as better than yourselves. Instead of each person watching out for their own good, watch out for what is better for others.

Philippians 2:3–4 CEB

But if we live in the light in the same way that God is in the light, we have a relationship with each other. And the blood of his Son Jesus cleanses us from every sin.

1 John 1:7 GW

If one part of the body suffers, all the other parts share its suffering. If one part is praised, all the others share in its happiness.

1 Corinthians 12:26 GW

That is why you are no longer foreigners and outsiders but citizens together with God's people and members of God's family. You are built on the foundation of the apostles and prophets. Christ Jesus himself is the cornerstone. In him all the parts of the building fit together and grow into a holy temple in the Lord. Through him you, also, are being built in the Spirit together with others into a place where God lives.

Ephesians 2:19–22 GW

SWEET REST

Dear Lord,

Thank You that You advise me through Your Word, as well as through the quiet words Your Spirit speaks to my heart. Sometimes people don't understand how I can hear Your voice, but as I lie on my bed thinking of You, meditating on Your Word, You give me clear instructions that speak into my inner depths. It's easy to recognize Your voice because it never opposes or betrays Your Word. Your instructions never break Your commandments. So when You speak to me, I will follow You, asking that You take the lead in all my steps so I can stop tripping over myself.

How happy my heart is as I celebrate You, how joyful my mood. How easy it is to rest in Your safety.

When I'm weary and burdened, You ask me to come to You so that You can give me rest. Because I'm yoked with You, I know Your gentleness and humble heart. You give me rest for my soul and make my steps light.

Tonight, I will sleep secure on a bed of peace because I know that You, the Eternal One, are always with me. You will protect me.

You will keep my mind in perfect peace as I continue to focus on You. This focus creates trust, and this trust fills my heart with peace. How joyful I am that this is the way You gift me with sweet rest.

Thank You, Lord.

I will bless the LORD who advises me;
even at night I am instructed
in the depths of my mind.
I always put the LORD in front of me;
I will not stumble because he is on my right side.
That's why my heart celebrates and my mood is joyous;
yes, my whole body will rest in safety.

Psalm 16:7–9 CEB

Come to Me, all who are weary and burdened, and I will give you rest. Take My yoke upon you and learn from Me, for I am gentle and humble in heart, and you will find rest for your souls. For My yoke is comfortable, and My burden is light.

Matthew 11:28–30 NASB

Tonight I will sleep securely on a bed of peace
because I trust You, You alone, O Eternal One, will
keep me safe.

Psalm 4:8 VOICE

And He said, "My presence shall go with you, and I will give you rest."

Exodus 33:14 NASB

You will keep the man in perfect peace whose mind is kept on You, because he trusts in You.

Isaiah 26:3 NLV

TRUSTING GOD

Dear Lord,

Why trust in my own plans when I can confidently put my trust in You?

The act of trusting You is like a tree pushing its hidden roots into pools of deep waters. Its branches become rich with cool, green shade. This tree will not wilt even on the hottest of days.

When I live with my roots in You, I flourish. My life produces fruit that will honor You and nourish others.

So, with joy, I commit my ways to You and watch You act on my behalf. You are an endless stream of cool water for my soul. That's why I can trust You to direct my life. As You do, I can only rejoice when You turn my problems into solutions and my difficulties into marvels.

I will have so much faith in You that it will become easy to believe You've already answered my prayer requests even before I finish praying. What joy as I watch You respond to my needs by fulfilling my requests in such beautiful, loving ways.

Thank You, Lord.

Place your trust in the Eternal; rely on Him completely;
never depend upon your own ideas and inventions.

Proverbs 3:5 VOICE

Blessed is the person who trusts the LORD.
The LORD will be his confidence.
He will be like a tree that is planted by water.
It will send its roots down to a stream.
It will not be afraid in the heat of summer.
Its leaves will turn green.
It will not be anxious during droughts.
It will not stop producing fruit.

Jeremiah 17:7–8 GW

Commit your way to the LORD;
trust in him, and he will act.

Psalm 37:5 ESV

That's why I tell you to have faith that you have already received whatever you pray for, and it will be yours.

Mark 11:24 GW

YIELDING TO YOUR SPIRIT

Dear Lord,

Before I met You, in the days when I had no understanding of the law of death, I gave myself to a life of sin and thought nothing of it. But now that my eyes have been opened to Your love, I can see You rescued me from the grip of sin that leads to eternal death. Now I want to be right with You. Please accept my gift of all of me. I set myself apart to live and work for You.

In return, You've given me the privilege of being filled with the Holy Spirit. As I walk with the Spirit, I can break free from the control of my fleshly desires. This means I no longer do whatever I want but will follow You wherever Your Spirit leads me. What joy that these attributes of a Spirit-led life are meant to be limitless.

When I live in and by Your Spirit, You produce such wonderful fruit in me, fruit that pours out of Your love. I have overflowing joy, peace that comforts my heart, patience that doesn't give up, loving-kindness, a life of goodness, faith that triumphs, gentleness of heart, and a strong spirit that no longer demands its own way.

None of these traits are against Your law, for through the power of Your Spirit, these gifts have no boundaries and can blossom wherever I go.

Thank You, Lord.

At one time you gave yourselves over to the power of sin. You kept on sinning all the more. Now give yourselves over to being right with God. Set yourself apart for God-like living and to do His work.

Romans 6:19 NLV

So I say, walk by the Spirit, and you will not gratify the desires of the flesh. For the flesh desires what is contrary to the Spirit, and the Spirit what is contrary to the flesh. They are in conflict with each other, so that you are not to do whatever you want. But if you are led by the Spirit, you are not under the law.

Galatians 5:16–18 NIV

But the fruit produced by the Holy Spirit within you is divine love in all its varied expressions: joy that overflows, peace that subdues, patience that endures, kindness in action, a life full of virtue, faith that prevails, gentleness of heart, and strength of spirit. Never set the law above these qualities, for they are meant to be limitless.

Galatians 5:22–23 TPT

Give thanks in all circumstances; for this is God's will for you in Christ Jesus.

1 Thessalonians 5:18 NIV

As long as thanks is possible, then joy is always possible. *Joy is always possible. Whenever*, meaning—now; *wherever*, meaning—here.

Ann Voskamp

FINDING JOY IN THE LORD

Dear Lord,

You are my joy and delight! You've dressed me in the shining robes of the salvation of Jesus to cover my filthy rags. I'm like a bridegroom in his finery, like a bride radiant in a gown covered in glimmering jewels.

I stand before You, glowing in Your love because You've dried my tears and invited me into a dance of praise. The barrier that once divided us has vanished through the power of Jesus Christ. Now my sin no longer separates me from You, the holy God. Not only did You lift the divider, You transformed my heartache into garments of gladness set aglow in the light of Your love.

I'm finally safe in You, and I rejoice with a song of joy. My happiness is found in You as You protect me with Your love.

You teach me endurance so whenever I run into trouble, I continue my race in Your power. My newfound endurance has turned me into a person with strength of character, whose confidence is in You, my salvation.

Thank You, Lord.

I will find joy in the LORD.
I will delight in my God.
He has dressed me in the clothes of salvation.
He has wrapped me in the robe of righteousness
like a bridegroom with a priest's turban,
like a bride with her jewels.

Isaiah 61:10 GW

You did it: You turned my deepest pains into joyful
dancing;
You stripped off my dark clothing
and covered me with joyful light.

Psalm 30:11 VOICE

But all who find safety in you will rejoice;
they can always sing for joy.
Protect those who love you;
because of you they are truly happy.

Psalm 5:11 GNT

We can rejoice, too, when we run into problems and trials, for we know that they help us develop endurance. And endurance develops strength of character, and character strengthens our confident hope of salvation.

Romans 5:3–4 NLT

GIVING

Dear Lord,

If life were a race to gain the most possessions, the winner's circle would contain a pile of trash next to an engraved tombstone. The winner's earthly goods would be sold, given away, or buried in a garbage heap.

But Your revelation about riches is that joy is not about the accumulation of things; joy is found in the pursuit of giving.

In fact, the more I give without wishing I could keep my cash, the more my giving pleases You. My generosity becomes an act of pure joy, a joy You, Lord, share with me.

As long as my gifts flow from my heart, they don't even need a price tag. The list of things you suggest I give to others includes love, peace, and forgiveness (with forgiveness being a prized treasure). When I forgive freely, Your grace and forgiveness expand to cover me. For You forgive me in the same measure that I forgive others.

The power of giving and forgiving is the same power as planting a crop. The more seeds of generosity I plant, the more I will gather. But if I'm stingy with the seeds You've given to me, there won't be much of a harvest. The rule is that the more I give, the wealthier I become in You. The stingier I am, the less I have in both pocket and soul.

This is because You promise that the generous will prosper and those who refresh others will themselves be refreshed.

Empower me to give with joy so that I can be empowered with joy!

Thank You, Lord.

We should remember the words that the Lord Jesus said, "Giving gifts is more satisfying than receiving them."

Acts 20:35 GW

Each man should give as he has decided in his heart. He should not give, wishing he could keep it. Or he should not give if he feels he has to give. God loves a man who gives because he wants to give.

2 Corinthians 9:7 NLV

Don't hold back—give freely, and you'll have plenty poured back into your lap—a good measure, pressed down, shaken together, brimming over. You'll receive in the same measure you give.

Luke 6:38 VOICE

Remember, the man who plants only a few seeds will not have much grain to gather. The man who plants many seeds will have much grain to gather.

2 Corinthians 9:6 NLV

Give freely and become more wealthy;
be stingy and lose everything.

The generous will prosper;
those who refresh others will themselves be refreshed.

Proverbs 11:24–25 NLT

GRATEFUL HEART

Dear Lord,

Create in me a grateful heart, a heart that sees Your miracles hidden inside my pain.

Whatever is good and perfect is a gift that comes from You, the Creator of the lights that fill the heavens. You are the Holy One, who never changes or shifts like a shadow.

Because of who You are, I can give thanks for everything in my life, both the good and the difficult. Giving thanks is Your will for me in Christ Jesus.

Because of Your kindness toward me, I praise You, Lord, with my whole being and soul.

Father, I thank You for all You've put in my life—yes, for everything—in the name of my Lord Jesus Christ. I will bring my constant praise to God the Father because of my joy of what Christ has done for me.

May all that I do, every word that I say, be in honor of my Lord Jesus, the One who loves me.

Thank You, Lord.

Whatever is good and perfect is a gift coming down to us from God our Father, who created all the lights in the heavens. He never changes or casts a shifting shadow.

James 1:17 NLT

Give thanks in all circumstances; for this is God's will for you in Christ Jesus.

1 Thessalonians 5:18 NIV

Praise the LORD, my soul,
and do not forget how kind he is.

Psalm 103:2 GNT

Always thank God the Father for everything in the name of our Lord Jesus Christ.

Ephesians 5:20 GW

Whatever you do [no matter what it is] in word or deed, do everything in the name of the Lord Jesus [and in dependence on Him], giving thanks to God the Father through Him.

Colossians 3:17 AMP

INVITING GOD INTO MY DAY

Dear Lord,

I've discovered that the secret to having more of You in my life is prayer, meaning telling You about my joys and needs, just as I would tell a friend. For that's what You are, the God who is my friend, the God who walks with me.

So, daily, I will call out to You, seeking You, Your strength, and Your presence now and always.

Because I call out to You, I do not need to be anxious about anything. And the fact that You long to hear my requests makes it so much easier to talk to you. As I tell You about my needs, I thank You for what You are already doing.

There are times I'm afraid to approach You or call out to You. Help me to always remember that I can call out to You any time of every day.

When I call, I will call in the name of Jesus so I can receive Your forgiveness and blessings with joy.

I'm confident that You listen to my prayer requests.

And while I ask for good things, I will remember to turn away from evil, and repent whenever I make a misstep. This prayer keeps the channel between us open so I can hear from You and so You will forgive my sins and make my life prosperous.

Thank You that my daily prayers connect us in Your love, peace, and guidance.

Thank You, Lord.

Seek the Lord and his strength;
seek his presence continually!

1 Chronicles 16:11 ESV

Don't be anxious about things; instead, pray. Pray about everything. He longs to hear your requests, so talk to God about your needs and be thankful for what has come.

Philippians 4:6 VOICE

So far you haven't asked for anything in my name. Ask and you will receive so that you can be completely happy.

John 16:24 GW

The Lord's eyes are on the righteous
and his ears are open to their prayers.

1 Peter 3:12 CEB

If they pray to me and repent and turn away from the evil they have been doing, then I will hear them in heaven, forgive their sins, and make their land prosperous again.

2 Chronicles 7:14 GNT

JOY CHALLENGE

Dear Lord,

Following Jesus is not always easy, for it comes with a price tag. If I want to walk with You, I must say no to many things I'd like to have or do. Instead of following my whims, I must pick up my cross and let You lead the way. If I decide to save my life, I will lose it. But if I lose my life in You, I will find it. What good would it do for me to have everything I've ever wanted if it costs me my life? The real question may be this: What am I willing to give You in exchange for my life?

The answer is, I'm willing to give You all of me, even my every whim.

Jesus told us not to be surprised at the painful tests we will suffer. He explained that suffering through tests is not unusual.

So, instead of being taken aback by what You allow in my life, I will trust You and be glad to share in the sufferings of Jesus. This is the path to greater joy, which reveals Your glory.

With this hope, I'm happy, even though times of sorrow and testing come. Tests prove my faith and show me Your goodness as You refine me like gold. You remove my impurities so my faith in You can grow and bring thanksgiving as well as greatness and honor to Jesus Christ.

So, even in my tests, I will find joy on my path. I will rejoice, pray, and offer thanksgiving through my tests, for this is Your will for my life as I serve Christ Jesus.

Thank You, Lord.

Then Jesus said to his disciples, "Those who want to come with me must say no to the things they want, pick up their crosses, and follow me. Those who want to save their lives will lose them. But those who lose their lives for me will find them. What good will it do for people to win the whole world and lose their lives? Or what will a person give in exchange for life?"

Matthew 16:24–26 GW

My dear friends, do not be surprised at the painful test you are suffering, as though something unusual were happening to you. Rather be glad that you are sharing Christ's sufferings, so that you may be full of joy when his glory is revealed.

1 Peter 4:12–13 GNT

With this hope you can be happy even if you need to have sorrow and all kinds of tests for awhile. These tests have come to prove your faith and to show that it is good. Gold, which can be destroyed, is tested by fire. Your faith is worth much more than gold and it must be tested also. Then your faith will bring thanks and shining-greatness and honor to Jesus Christ when He comes again.

1 Peter 1:6–7 NLV

Rejoice always, pray continually, give thanks in all circumstances; for this is God's will for you in Christ Jesus.

1 Thessalonians 5:16–18 NIV

JOYFUL HEART

Dear Lord,

When I entertain sorrow, my strength is zapped. But when I remember that You are with me, I'm filled with joy—a joy that renews my strength. Your strength empowers me to be resilient so I can rise above my troubles.

When I think of You instead of my disappointments, I can skip my pity party and accept Your invitation to trust You as You turn my disappointments into joy.

I'm awed that You, the Lord Most High, would even care to listen to me. But You do! This makes You my hero, a hero who saves me and rejoices over me.

I'm amazed that my Creator is glad to know me and delights in my love for Him. How can my heart be troubled when I've found such love and grace?

Lord, You renew me with Your love and celebrate me with shouts of joy.

It's astounding to know that like a mom cradling her beloved child, You sing a song of love over me.

With my heart filled with gratitude, it is easy to keep my joy intact. And because You are with me, I will constantly share my heart and needs with You. I will trust You and thank You for my every circumstance. Because I belong to You, Jesus Christ, I know You have a plan to work out every difficulty for my good.

You do this because You love me. And because You love me, I love You right back.

Thank You, Lord.

A joyful heart is good medicine,
but depression drains one's strength.

Proverbs 17:22 GW

Don't be sad because the joy you have in the Lord is your strength.

Nehemiah 8:10 GW

The Lord your God is with you.
He is a hero who saves you.
He happily rejoices over you,
renews you with his love,
and celebrates over you with shouts of joy.

Zephaniah 3:17 GW

Always be joyful. Never stop praying. Be thankful in all circumstances, for this is God's will for you who belong to Christ Jesus.

1 Thessalonians 5:16–18 NLT

We know that all things work together for the good of those who love God—those whom he has called according to his plan.

Romans 8:28 GW

JOY THAT ENDURES

Dear Lord,

I know I can endure this race because You promise I can do all things through Christ who strengthens me.

I can run with endurance the course before me as all of heaven cheers me on. This knowledge makes it easier to cast off my baggage and kick away any sin that could trip me.

I fix my eyes on the finish line, my door to eternity with You. That's why I will run and not lose heart. Even when I feel I'm losing ground, I know You are with me, renewing my strength. You restore my faith so I can finish well. So, when I step into potholes or face roadblocks, I know the victory will be worth every jarring pain and delay.

I celebrate leg cramps, sore muscles, and all pain I'm experiencing, because pain means I'm enduring, which means I'm moving closer to the finish line.

My endurance makes me stronger and more determined. It helps me to learn to hope and anticipate Your goodness.

May I never grow tired of pressing on, doing what is good in Your eyes. Because in season, many runners will be inspired and follow my footsteps. Help us anticipate the joy we will feel as we cross the finish line into the arms of Jesus.

Thank You, Lord.

I can do everything through Christ who strengthens me.

Philippians 4:13 GW

So then, with endurance, let's also run the race that is laid out in front of us, since we have such a great cloud of witnesses surrounding us. Let's throw off any extra baggage, get rid of the sin that trips us up.

Hebrews 12:1 CEB

Therefore we do not lose heart. Though outwardly we are wasting away, yet inwardly we are being renewed day by day. For our light and momentary troubles are achieving for us an eternal glory that far outweighs them all. So we fix our eyes not on what is seen, but on what is unseen, since what is seen is temporary, but what is unseen is eternal.

2 Corinthians 4:16–18 NIV

And that's not all. We also celebrate in seasons of suffering because we know that when we suffer we develop endurance, which shapes our characters. When our characters are refined, we learn what it means to hope and anticipate God's goodness.

Romans 5:3–4 VOICE

May we never tire of doing what is good and right before our Lord because in His season we shall bring in a great harvest if we can just persist.

Galatians 6:9 VOICE

JOY TRANSFORMATION

Dear Lord,

Here's a mystery: You want me to live in this world without adapting to its norms. I'm not to conform but to be transformed, renewing my mind with Your Word. I'm to find and establish Your good, perfect, and pleasing will for my life. I don't need to take a shot in the dark concerning my purpose because I can rely on Your guidance.

Because I am a believer in Christ, You've made me a new creation, a human with the Spirit of the living God resting in my heart. With You so entwined in my life, how could I continue with my old lifestyle? Teach me how to walk into this new way of living You've set before me.

Besides making me a new creation, You've given me a new heart and placed the Holy Spirit inside of me, turning my heart of stone into a heart filled with love.

Thank You that You are completing this work You started so I will be ready for the day of Jesus Christ.

Not only have You transformed me, You've transformed multitudes, lifting the poor from the dust, the needy from the garbage dump, and allowing them to rub shoulders with royalty.

You give the childless woman a family and make her a mother.

You have made my barren heart a place filled with love so that I can share it with those You've given me.

Thank You, Lord.

Do not conform to the pattern of this world, but be transformed by the renewing of your mind. Then you will be able to test and approve what God's will is—his good, pleasing and perfect will.

Romans 12:2 NIV

Whoever is a believer in Christ is a new creation. The old way of living has disappeared. A new way of living has come into existence.

2 Corinthians 5:17 GW

And I will give you a new heart, and I will put a new spirit in you. I will take out your stony, stubborn heart and give you a tender, responsive heart.

Ezekiel 36:26 NLT

And I am sure of this, that he who began a good work in you will bring it to completion at the day of Jesus Christ.

Philippians 1:6 ESV

He lifts the poor from the dust
and the needy from the garbage dump.
He sets them among princes,
even the princes of his own people!
He gives the childless woman a family,
making her a happy mother.

Praise the Lord!

Psalm 113:7–9 NLT

LIFTING NEEDS TO GOD

Dear Lord,

When I didn't know better, I dragged my neediness to every solution but You. How frustrating it was to face failure in every place I looked. But now I'm happy to hand my needs over to You. For I've learned that when I try to carry my needs myself, I stir up trouble and make things worse. But when I trust my needs to You, You create solutions I could never have imagined were possible.

As I trust You with my needs, I honor You with my obedience because You promise that those who obey You will have everything they need. Even wild lions go hungry in periods of drought, but the Word says those who obey You will never lack.

As I live for You by seeking the kingdom of God, Your Word promises that You will take care of everything.

Young David, the shepherd boy who watched over his flocks, discovered this truth about You and sang this song, "The LORD is my shepherd. I am never in need."

Just as You were David's Shepherd, You are my Shepherd. You supply my every need according to Your riches in glory in Christ Jesus.

So, thank You! Thank You for taking care of me. Thank You for being my Provider.

I'm happy that I'm Yours and that You are mine, for not only do You provide my needs, You give me the desires of my heart.

Thank You, Lord.

Honor the Lord, all his people;
those who obey him have all they need.
Even lions go hungry for lack of food,
but those who obey the Lord lack nothing good.

Psalm 34:9–10 GNT

Seek the Kingdom of God above all else, and live righteously, and he will give you everything you need.

Matthew 6:33 NLT

The Lord is my shepherd.
I am never in need.

Psalm 23:1 GW

And my God will supply every need of yours according to his riches in glory in Christ Jesus.

Philippians 4:19 ESV

Be happy with the Lord,
and he will give you the desires of your heart.

Psalm 37:4 GW

NEVER ALONE

Dear Lord,

You, the Eternal One, have encouraged me to be strong with strength of heart. You want me to live fearless, filled with faith. You promise to be with me and to protect me wherever I go.

People may try to oppose me, but because of Your power and protection, they don't stand a chance. This is because You will never fail or abandon me. For You are with me just as You were with Moses. You love me with the same love with which You loved Your Son, Jesus.

Whenever I lose sight of You, I will search for You, and when I search for You with all my heart, I will find You.

I pledge to abide in Your love. Living outside of Your love would be as if I were to chop a branch off a fig tree; that branch would wither and die, never producing fruit again.

In this same way, if I, the branch, am separated from You, I will not be able to bear fruit. But when I abide in You and You abide in me, I will burst forth in blossoms that will produce works of love. I am in You, and Your Spirit is alive in me. I joyfully live through the power of the Spirit, who empowers me to do all You have planned for me.

Thank You, Lord.

Have I not told you? Be strong and have strength of heart! Do not be afraid or lose faith. For the Lord your God is with you anywhere you go.

Joshua 1:9 NLV

No one will be able to oppose you for as long as you live. I will be with you just as I was with Moses, and I will never fail or abandon you.

Joshua 1:5 VOICE

When you search for me, yes, search for me with all your heart, you will find me.

Jeremiah 29:13 CEB

I have loved you the same way the Father has loved me. So live in my love.

John 15:9 GW

Abide in Me, and I will abide in you. A branch cannot bear fruit if it is disconnected from the vine, and neither will you if you are not connected to Me.

John 15:4 VOICE

He has given us His Spirit. This is how we live by His help and He lives in us.

1 John 4:13 NLV

OPEN DOORS TO JOY

Dear Lord,

Even though there are those who oppose me, You've given me the ability to rise above it and continue to do effective work.

I will accomplish that work because I have You and Your power. I will search for Your solutions and find them. I will knock on the door of serving others, and You will open it. I will ask for Your help, and I will receive it. For when I search, You give me the joy to find; when I knock, You give me the joy of an open door.

You also give me the keys of the kingdom of heaven. When I ask You to bind the work of the enemy, his work is bound in heaven; when I ask You to loose the work of the Spirit, the Spirit's work is loosed in heaven. So, I ask You to bind the enemy from the work You have given me and I ask You to loose the power of the Holy Spirit so that many will come into Your kingdom.

I see the open door You have placed in front of me. It's a door no one can shut because You are that door. I will enter in, for in You I'm saved and find my home. Even when I'm weak, You help me keep Your Word and strengthen me to praise Your name.

Thank You, Lord.

I have a great opportunity to do effective work here, although there are many people who oppose me.

1 Corinthians 16:9 GW

Ask, and you will receive. Search, and you will find. Knock, and the door will be opened for you. Everyone who asks will receive. The one who searches will find, and for the one who knocks, the door will be opened.

Matthew 7:7–8 GW

I will give you the keys of the kingdom of heaven, and whatever you bind on earth shall be bound in heaven, and whatever you loose on earth shall be loosed in heaven.

Matthew 16:19 ESV

I know your works. Look! I have set in front of you an open door that no one can shut. You have so little power, and yet you have kept my word and haven't denied my name.

Revelation 3:8 CEB

I am the door. If anyone enters by me, he will be saved and will go in and out and find pasture.

John 10:9 ESV

OVERCOMING

Dear Lord,

Thank You that I'm Your child and that I belong to You.

Because I believe Jesus is Your Son, You are alive inside of me.

As I'm not yet living in heaven but I exist in a world where the evil one prowls like a roaring lion, it's good that I'm empowered by the One who is greater than my enemy.

I live as a new creation in You, and because You're living in me, I overcome the world through Your power.

So why should I try to mold myself to be like those who live in darkness? Their way of living is not for me. Instead, You've given me the Holy Spirit's power so I can inwardly transform my thoughts and thinking. The bonus is, You empower me to discern Your will as I live a wonderful life, a life that You find good, pleasing, and complete.

So, with all this going for me, I refuse to be conquered by evil. Instead, I will conquer evil by doing good.

Thank You for sharing Your secrets with me through Your Word because this good news brings me peace. Knowing who I am in You has filled me with joy. How glad I am that my God, living in me, is the final champion!

Thank You, Lord.

Little children, you are from God and have overcome them, for he who is in you is greater than he who is in the world.

1 John 4:4 ESV

Who is it that overcomes the world except the one who believes that Jesus is the Son of God?

1 John 5:5 ESV

Do not allow this world to mold you in its own image. Instead, be transformed from the inside out by renewing your mind. As a result, you will be able to discern what God wills and whatever God finds good, pleasing, and complete.

Romans 12:2 VOICE

Don't let evil conquer you, but conquer evil by doing good.

Romans 12:21 NLT

I've told you this so that my peace will be with you. In the world you'll have trouble. But cheer up! I have overcome the world.

John 16:33 GW

PRESENCE OF THE HOLY SPIRIT

Dear Lord,

When I gave You my heart, I gave You my body too, which is now a temple filled with the presence of Your Holy Spirit. The presence of the Spirit is a gift from You, a gift that fills my soul.

This means I'm all in. I belong to You.

Because I love You and I have chosen to obey Your commandments, You sent me Your Holy Spirit, my Helper, to be with me forever.

The world can't accept the Spirit because the world is blind and can't see who He is! But, as I'm not of the world but of the kingdom of heaven, I'm aware of His presence! Your Spirit of truth is always with me, alive inside of me.

The Spirit empowers me to have a life full of love, joy, peace, perseverance, kindness, goodness, faith, and gentleness and teaches me how to tame my own desires. These gifts are not only beautiful but will never be against Your law.

The Spirit helps me in my weakness. When I have no idea what to pray, the Holy Spirit prays for me in wordless groans.

Lord, You are the source of my hope, You fill me with peace and endless joy. My hope overflows by the power of the Holy Spirit.

I'm blessed.

Thank You, Lord.

Don’t you know that your body is the temple of the Holy Spirit who comes from God and dwells inside of you? You do not own yourself.

1 Corinthians 6:19 VOICE

If you love me, you will obey my commandments. I will ask the Father, and he will give you another helper who will be with you forever. That helper is the Spirit of Truth. The world cannot accept him, because it doesn’t see or know him. You know him, because he lives with you and will be in you.

John 14:15–17 GW

But the fruit that comes from having the Holy Spirit in our lives is: love, joy, peace, not giving up, being kind, being good, having faith, being gentle, and being the boss over our own desires. The Law is not against these things.

Galatians 5:22–23 NLV

In the same way, the Spirit helps us in our weakness. We do not know what we ought to pray for, but the Spirit himself intercedes for us through wordless groans.

Romans 8:26 NIV

May God, the source of hope, fill you with joy and peace through your faith in him. Then you will overflow with hope by the power of the Holy Spirit.

Romans 15:13 GW

QUIET MOMENTS WITH GOD

Dear Lord,

Thank You for this quiet moment where I can turn my thoughts to the beauty of You. I breathe in and feel Your presence. I quiet my soul and feel Your love.

As I think of Your greatness and majesty, I tremble because I do not want to sin against You.

When I lie on my bed, You ask me to search my heart in silence. So I will be quiet and realize that You indeed are God.

The nations will honor You, and Your name will be honored on the whole earth.

I'm humbled by Your love. What joy that You fight for me, and all I have to do is keep my heart and worries still before You in quiet trust. So I will be still in Your presence, Lord. I will wait patiently for You to act, never giving a care about evil people who prosper. Neither will I fret about their wicked schemes.

I will wait with hope for You, Lord. I will be strong and my heart courageous. Yes, I will be quiet as I put my hope in You.

Thank You, Lord.

Tremble and do not sin;
when you are on your beds,
search your hearts and be silent.

Psalm 4:4 NIV

Be quiet and know that I am God. I will be honored among the nations. I will be honored in the earth.

Psalm 46:10 NLV

The Lord will fight for you, and all you have to do is keep still.

Exodus 14:14 GNT

Be still in the presence of the Lord,
and wait patiently for him to act.
Don't worry about evil people who prosper
or fret about their wicked schemes.

Psalm 37:7 NLT

Wait with hope for the Lord.
Be strong, and let your heart be courageous.
Yes, wait with hope for the Lord.

Psalm 27:14 GW

SHARING OUR FAITH

Dear Lord,

I love You and want to tell others about what You have done for me. Make a way so I can be heard. Bring me those who will listen and understand. Give me the courage to be bold so I can share with those who have yet to hear.

How can I be ashamed of Your wonderful message, which has the power to save anyone who turns to You? Give me divine appointments with those who don't know You yet so I can share that what You did for me You can also do for them. You lovingly make a way so that everyone who believes will be saved.

For You put a new song in my mouth, a song of praise to You. Many will see and fear and put their trust in You.

With joy, I dedicate my life to Christ the Lord. Whenever anyone asks me to explain it, I tell them of my confidence in You with gentleness and respect.

Jesus, You say I am the light of the world, and like a city on a hilltop, the message inside me cannot be hidden. Who turns on their flashlight and hides it in a drawer? Who unscrews an illuminated light bulb when they need to see in the dark? Who hides a candle in their refrigerator? A candle is placed in a holder so it can give light to all who gather around it.

So, in this same way, I will live a life shining with good deeds for all to see so that everyone will praise You, my heavenly Father.

Thank You, Lord.

Come and listen, all who honor God,
and I will tell you what he has done for me.

Psalm 66:16 GNT

I'm not ashamed of the Good News. It is God's power to save everyone who believes, Jews first and Greeks as well.

Romans 1:16 GW

He put a new song in my mouth,
a song of praise to our God.
Many will see and fear,
and put their trust in the Lord.

Psalm 40:3 ESV

But dedicate your lives to Christ as Lord. Always be ready to defend your confidence in God when anyone asks you to explain it. However, make your defense with gentleness and respect.

1 Peter 3:15 GW

You are the light of the world—like a city on a hilltop that cannot be hidden. No one lights a lamp and then puts it under a basket. Instead, a lamp is placed on a stand, where it gives light to everyone in the house. In the same way, let your good deeds shine out for all to see, so that everyone will praise your heavenly Father.

Matthew 5:14–16 NLT

SIMPLE THINGS OF LIFE

Dear Lord,

Why do I try to make faith so complicated when it's the simple act of trusting who You are?

As I trust You, You remind me to focus my thoughts on what is true, honorable, right, pure, lovely, and admirable. This means I need to quit focusing on worries that keep me from believing that my life is in Your hands. Help me to focus instead on the joy of the blessings You have given me.

One such blessing is that You are the center of my life. Therefore, I will live in simplicity and godly sincerity, not swayed by so-called earthly wisdom. Instead, I will live by Your grace, with You as my focus.

My life is not about loving worldly things; my life is about loving You. Worldly things like lust, envy, and pride are only poor and harmful substitutes for Your lovely gifts. The things that are the focus of my worldly desires will pass away, but I will live forever if I do Your will.

You have raised me from death to life through Christ. So, I will seek things that are above, where Christ is seated at Your right hand.

With joy, I will set my mind on heavenly things and quit running after the counterfeits of this world.

Thank You, Lord.

And now, dear brothers and sisters, one final thing. Fix your thoughts on what is true, and honorable, and right, and pure, and lovely, and admirable. Think about things that are excellent and worthy of praise.

Philippians 4:8 NLT

For our boast is this, the testimony of our conscience, that we behaved in the world with simplicity and godly sincerity, not by earthly wisdom but by the grace of God, and supremely so toward you.

2 Corinthians 1:12 ESV

Do not love the world or anything in the world. If anyone loves the world, love for the Father is not in them. For everything in the world—the lust of the flesh, the lust of the eyes, and the pride of life—comes not from the Father but from the world. The world and its desires pass away, but whoever does the will of God lives forever.

1 John 2:15–17 NIV

If then you have been raised with Christ, seek the things that are above, where Christ is, seated at the right hand of God. Set your minds on things that are above, not on things that are on earth.

Colossians 3:1–2 ESV

WALKING IN FAITH

Dear Lord,

Walking in faith is not like walking blindfolded; instead, it's like following the glow of Your light as it illuminates my every step. Just because You don't provide a highlighted road map for my journey, it doesn't mean You aren't guiding me. For You are my guiding light of love, a light I can trust.

I have so enjoyed trusting in Your loving-kindness. My heart is full of joy because I know You not only guide me but also save me.

For it is by grace You save me through faith. This isn't anything I did for myself; this salvation is a gift from You. It was not earned by my good works.

My faith is a deep confidence and assurance that what I hope for in You will come to pass. What joy that I do not need to worry as I trust in You.

Even though I've never seen You, I love You. Because I believe in You, I'm filled with an inexpressible and glorious joy.

So, I will trust You, Lord, with all my heart because I'm in Your hands.

I turn all my worries over to You, for You will make my paths straight.

Thank You, Lord.

But I have trusted in Your loving-kindness. My heart will be full of joy because You will save me.

Psalm 13:5 NLV

For it is by grace you have been saved, through faith—and this is not from yourselves, it is the gift of God—not by works, so that no one can boast.

Ephesians 2:8–9 NIV

Now faith is confidence in what we hope for and assurance about what we do not see.

Hebrews 11:1 NIV

Though you have not seen him, you love him; and even though you do not see him now, you believe in him and are filled with an inexpressible and glorious joy.

1 Peter 1:8 NIV

Trust in the Lord with all your heart
and lean not on your own understanding;
in all your ways submit to him,
and he will make your paths straight.

Proverbs 3:5–6 NIV

WALKING WITH JESUS

Dear Lord,

As I learn how You were born of a virgin, lived a sinless life, loved the people and disciples who gathered around You, and laid down Your life on the cross as a payment for the sin of humankind, I can't help but marvel. And knowing that You, the sinless One, resurrected from death to life to rescue me from sin and death, I can only thank You. I bow before You, my Lord, my Savior.

I will listen for Your voice. I will recognize it because Your voice is a voice of love. You know me, and I follow You.

You ask that I come to You when I'm tired of carrying a heavy load. You promise to give me rest. So, with joy, I follow Your teachings and learn from You. For You are gentle, You are without pride, and You give me rest for my soul. When I'm yoked to You, my load is easy and my burdens are light.

For You are the light of the world, and because I follow You, I will never walk in darkness. How can darkness overcome me when I have You, the Light of Life?

I have put my trust in You, my Lord Jesus Christ. You took my punishment for sin, and You saved me. I will follow You wherever You take me.

Give me Your power to keep Your Word so that I may be perfected by Your love. That way, others will know I am in You. Lead me in how to walk as You walked as I continue to abide in You.

Thank You, Lord.

My sheep listen to my voice; I know them, and they follow me.

John 10:27 GNT

Come to Me, all of you who work and have heavy loads. I will give you rest. Follow My teachings and learn from Me. I am gentle and do not have pride. You will have rest for your souls. For My way of carrying a load is easy and My load is not heavy.

Matthew 11:28–30 NLV

Jesus spoke to all the people, saying, "I am the Light of the world. Anyone who follows Me will not walk in darkness. He will have the Light of Life."

John 8:12 NLV

As you have put your trust in Christ Jesus the Lord to save you from the punishment of sin, now let Him lead you in every step.

Colossians 2:6 NLV

But whoever keeps his word, in him truly the love of God is perfected. By this we may know that we are in him: whoever says he abides in him ought to walk in the same way in which he walked.

1 John 2:5–6 ESV

WORSHIP INTO *joy*

Shout for joy to the LORD, all the earth.
Worship the LORD with gladness;
come before him with joyful songs.

Psalm 100:1–2 NIV

We should thank God for every stream of joy in our lives while recognizing that Christ is the ocean from which every stream flows.

Randy Alcorn

ANSWERED PRAYER

Dear Lord,

Prayer used to be something I dreaded because I wasn't sure I was good enough to talk to You. But that was before I understood who I am. Now I see that I live in You and Your Word lives in me, meaning I'm now a new creature in Christ. My Christ-identity gives me the privilege of coming to You with anything I want, knowing that You will hear me. The amazing thing is, according to Your Word, You will give me whatever I ask.

In the face of this truth, I have no need to be anxious. I can come to You in prayer with a thankful heart, knowing without a doubt that You hear and will answer my requests.

So I wait patiently for You with my pleas, with the realization that You have turned Your face to me because I have called to You.

I will rejoice and pray without ceasing, thanking You for Your good gifts. My grateful attitude is Your will for me because I am in Christ, who is the giver of all things good.

I never give my own children evil gifts but good things. So how much more will You, my heavenly Father, the ultimate gift giver, give good gifts to me when I ask?

My heart is full because You hear me and answer me with good.

Thank You, Lord.

If you live in me and what I say lives in you, then ask for anything you want, and it will be yours.

John 15:7 GW

Do not be anxious about anything, but in everything by prayer and pleading with thanksgiving let your requests be made known to God.

Philippians 4:6 NASB

I waited patiently for the Lord.
He turned to me and heard my cry for help.

Psalm 40:1 GW

Rejoice always, pray without ceasing, in everything give thanks; for this is the will of God for you in Christ Jesus.

1 Thessalonians 5:16–18 NASB

If you who are evil know how to give good gifts to your children, how much more will your heavenly Father give good things to those who ask him.

Matthew 7:11 CEB

AWESOMENESS OF GOD

Dear Lord,

Your awesomeness is greater than I could ever imagine. When I praise You with my whole heart, I glimpse Your glory and my heart bursts with joy.

For You are the God of heaven and You are great. You are the God who keeps His covenant of unfailing love with me—because I love and obey You.

I worship You, for You alone are the Lord. You are the Creator of the universe, the One who made the skies and the heavens. Even the stars in the sky sing to You. You made the earth and the seas and everything in them, and You preserve them all. The angels sing their hallelujahs to You!

I praise You, my awesome God. Though You are in heaven, You are in this moment with me. You give me and all Your people power and strength.

You are the God of gods and the Lord of lords—great, mighty, and awesome. You love me as much as You love each of Your children. There is no bribe that would tempt You to remove Your love from me.

Thank You for living in the temple of my heart. Thank You for abiding with me. My heart and my flesh sing for joy to You, the living God.

Thank You, Lord.

Then I said, "O LORD, God of heaven, the great and awesome God who keeps his covenant of unfailing love with those who love him and obey his commands."

Nehemiah 1:5 NLT

You alone are the LORD. You made the skies and the heavens and all the stars. You made the earth and the seas and everything in them. You preserve them all, and the angels of heaven worship you.

Nehemiah 9:6 NLT

You, God, are awesome in your sanctuary;
the God of Israel gives power and strength to his people.

Praise be to God!

Psalm 68:35 NIV

For the LORD your God is the God of gods and Lord of lords. He is the great God, the mighty and awesome God, who shows no partiality and cannot be bribed.

Deuteronomy 10:17 NLT

How beautiful are the places where You live, O Lord of all! My soul wants and even becomes weak from wanting to be in the house of the Lord. My heart and my flesh sing for joy to the living God.

Psalm 84:1–2 NLV

BEAUTY OF GOD'S CREATION

Dear Lord,

How I love to praise You, the Creator of all. How glad that I'm part of Your creation. For Your creation is beautiful and wonderfully made. With joy, I lift my arms and worship You.

I shout with joy to You, the Lord of all the earth. I worship You with gladness and come before You with joyful songs. For You are worthy to receive glory and honor and power.

You are the Creator who created all things. By Your will all things were created and have their being. Even the sky reveals Your glory and glows with the work You have done.

Because of who You are, I will go out in joy and be led forth in peace. The mountains and hills will burst into song before You. The trees of the field will clap their hands.

How joyful to join in with creation's worship, to worship the One who created even me.

Thank You, Lord.

Shout for joy to the LORD, all the earth.
  Worship the LORD with gladness;
  come before him with joyful songs.

Psalm 100:1–2 NIV

You are worthy, our Lord and God,
  to receive glory and honor and power,
for you created all things,
  and by your will they were created
  and have their being.

Revelation 4:11 NIV

How clearly the sky reveals God's glory!
  How plainly it shows what he has done!

Psalm 19:1 GNT

You will go out in joy
  and be led forth in peace;
the mountains and hills
  will burst into song before you,
and all the trees of the field
  will clap their hands.

Isaiah 55:12 NIV

EMPOWERING GOD

Dear Lord,

I'm so small compared to this world of struggles. Just when I think I'm not going to make it, the words of Jesus ring in my soul. He said that His grace was enough for me, that His power was made perfect in my weakness. This means that my weakness is a necessary ingredient in the miracles that are coming into my life. I will never be able to take credit for even one of these blessings. This is why I will boast gladly in my weakness, so the power of Christ can rest on me.

The power of the Holy Spirit has come upon me, and I'm anointed to tell others the good news of salvation, including my family, my neighbors, and those You have put into my life.

I even have the authority to crush snakes and scorpions under my feet. I have authority over all the power of the enemy. Nothing will harm me.

I don't rejoice because the spirits submit to me; I rejoice because God has written my name in the Lamb's Book of Life. I rejoice that I can be with You forever.

Thank You for Your gifts from the wealth of Your glory. Please also give me inner strength and power through Your Holy Spirit.

For though I grow older by the day, and even though my body and heart may grow weak, You, my God, are the strength of my heart, and You are all I need forever.

Thank You, Lord.

But he said to me, “My grace is sufficient for you, for my power is made perfect in weakness.” Therefore I will boast all the more gladly of my weaknesses, so that the power of Christ may rest upon me.

2 Corinthians 12:9 ESV

But you will receive power when the Holy Spirit has come upon you, and you will be my witnesses in Jerusalem and in all Judea and Samaria, and to the end of the earth.

Acts 1:8 ESV

Look, I have given you authority to crush snakes and scorpions underfoot. I have given you authority over all the power of the enemy. Nothing will harm you. Nevertheless, don't rejoice because the spirits submit to you. Rejoice instead that your names are written in heaven.

Luke 10:19–20 CEB

I'm asking God to give you a gift from the wealth of his glory. I pray that he would give you inner strength and power through his Spirit.

Ephesians 3:16 GW

My body and my heart may grow weak, but God is the strength of my heart and all I need forever.

Psalm 73:26 NLV

ENCAMPED AROUND ME

Dear Lord,

It's amazing that You are faithful to me when I'm the one who needs to be more faithful to You. In Your faithfulness, You determine my steps so I will not walk into trouble. You guard me from the evil one so I can hide in You.

You wrap me with Yourself, and when evil tries to catch me in its snare, You deliver me.

You have me surrounded on every side. Not only are You behind me, You go before me with Your hand on my shoulder, giving me assurance of Your presence. You know me deeply, inside and out. It's so amazing how You, the Mighty God, are so near to me that I can hardly wrap my mind around it.

It's a good thing I'm not on the lam from You, because You see me wherever I go. I can never hide from Your Spirit or escape from Your watchful presence.

Just as David, the shepherd-king, explained when he said that You were always before him, You are always before me too. You were at David's right hand so he could not be shaken. You are at my right hand as well, and nothing can shake me because of Your presence.

Like David, my heart is glad that You are with me, so I praise You with joy. Your presence helps me rest with hope.

Surround me with Your faithful love, because I will always wait patiently for You, Your help, and Your guidance. My trust is in You.

Thank You, Lord.

But the Lord is faithful. He will establish you and guard you against the evil one.

2 Thessalonians 3:3 ESV

The angel of the Lord encamps around those who fear him,
and he delivers them.

Psalm 34:7 NIV

You have surrounded me on every side, behind me and before me,
and You have placed Your hand gently on my shoulder.
It is the most amazing feeling to know how deeply You know me, inside and out;
the realization of it is so great that I cannot comprehend it.

Can I go anywhere apart from Your Spirit?
Is there anywhere I can go to escape Your watchful presence?

Psalm 139:5–7 VOICE

David said about him:

"I saw the Lord always before me.
Because he is at my right hand,
I will not be shaken.
Therefore my heart is glad and my tongue rejoices;
my body also will rest in hope."

Acts 2:25–26 NIV

Lord, let your faithful love surround us
because we wait for you.

Psalm 33:22 CEB

ENCOUNTERING CHRIST

Dear Lord,

What a marvelous thing that I can encounter Christ.

Jesus promises that all who ask will receive, all who search will find, and all who knock will stand before an open door.

So, Lord, I ask to receive Jesus, I seek Your will for my life, I knock on Your door to enter into fellowship with You. You respond to my appeals by giving me access to You through Jesus, by opening the door so I can know You.

Because I repent of my sin and ask You to come into my life, Lord, I become a brand-new person with a fresh life filled with You.

Jesus told the woman at the well that He could give her living water. Please give me Your living water as well. As I drink of it, my spirit will never thirst, for I will be like a fresh, bubbling spring, a well of eternal life.

I rejoice because of all that You have accomplished for me through Jesus. Because of His work on the cross to cover my sin and shame, I can now walk with You. Jesus has made a way for You to be my friend.

I know I will suffer because of my faith, but I'm happy to share in this suffering because it is only a taste of the suffering that Jesus endured for me on the cross. Through Your power and shining-greatness, I will overcome and be filled with great joy.

Thank You, Lord.

Ask, and you will receive. Search, and you will find. Knock, and the door will be opened for you. Everyone who asks will receive. The one who searches will find, and for the one who knocks, the door will be opened.

Matthew 7:7–8 GW

When someone becomes a Christian, he becomes a brand new person inside. He is not the same anymore. A new life has begun!

2 Corinthians 5:17 TLB

Jesus replied, "Anyone who drinks this water will soon become thirsty again. But those who drink the water I give will never be thirsty again. It becomes a fresh, bubbling spring within them, giving them eternal life."

John 4:13–14 NLT

But that is not all; we rejoice because of what God has done through our Lord Jesus Christ, who has now made us God's friends.

Romans 5:11 GNT

Be happy that you are able to share some of the suffering of Christ. When His shining-greatness is shown, you will be filled with much joy.

1 Peter 4:13 NLV

GOD MY HELPER

Dear Lord,

When I look toward the mountains, searching for help, I remember that my help comes from You, the Maker of heaven and earth.

It is no small thing that the Creator of the universe would stoop to hear my cry.

But You, the God of love, are my light and my salvation.

Therefore, I have no need to fear anyone or anything. For You are the fortress protecting my life from the schemes of the enemy.

As Jesus promised, You sent Your Holy Spirit in the name of Jesus—to me. Me! The Spirit teaches and reminds me of the words of Jesus to help me trust Him.

Jesus is my High Priest, the One who offers the sacrificial lamb to God to cover my sins. Not only is Jesus my Priest, but He is also my Sacrificial Lamb, slain for my sin. Through His work on the cross, Jesus covers my sins with His own blood.

My High Priest understands my weaknesses, as He faced the same testings as I do, yet unlike me, He never sinned. In this way, He became the perfect, sinless Lamb, a Lamb without spot.

Because of the sacrifice of Jesus, I can come boldly to the throne of my gracious God in the name of Your Son. I rejoice, for there I will receive Your mercy and find Your grace to help me when I need it most.

For You are my refuge, my ever-present help in times of trouble.

Thank You, Lord.

I look up toward the mountains.
Where can I find help?
My help comes from the Lord,
the maker of heaven and earth.

Psalm 121:1–2 GW

The Lord is my light and my salvation.
Should I fear anyone?
The Lord is a fortress protecting my life.
Should I be frightened of anything?

Psalm 27:1 CEB

But the Helper, the Holy Spirit, whom the Father will send in my name, he will teach you all things and bring to your remembrance all that I have said to you.

John 14:26 ESV

This High Priest of ours understands our weaknesses, for he faced all of the same testings we do, yet he did not sin. So let us come boldly to the throne of our gracious God. There we will receive his mercy, and we will find grace to help us when we need it most.

Hebrews 4:15–16 NLT

God is our refuge and strength,
an ever-present help in times of trouble.

Psalm 46:1 GW

JOY GIVER

Dear Lord,

You are my joy giver. Even when my soul is weary, You remind me that this day is holy to You. You instruct me not to grieve, for Your joy is my strength. Please help me to stop focusing on my worries and turn my attention to all the ways You have blessed me.

The fastest way for me to regain my joy is to give thanks to You.

Even when I fail You, You turn away Your anger and comfort me. I will trust You and not be afraid. For You are my strength and my song. You are the One who saves me.

When the disciples thought they lost You to death on the cross, the world rejoiced while they mourned. But three days later, You walked into the upper room where they hid from the world. How they rejoiced to see that You were alive from the dead.

Just as it was with Your victory over death on the cross, You give me victory over the death of my hopes and dreams, as well as victory regarding what seems like unanswered prayer. That's because when I release my requests and heartaches by trusting in You, You turn my requests and troubles into miracles and my heartaches into joy.

May I always come to You in joy, with a glad heart. May I always remember to be thankful for Your salvation. May I always tell the good news of Your greatness.

You've revealed Your path of life to me, and I find complete joy in Your presence. You provide me with joy because You are by my side, now and forever.

Thank You, Lord.

This day is holy to our Lord. Do not grieve, for the joy of the LORD is your strength.

Nehemiah 8:10 NIV

You will say on that day, "I will give thanks to You, O Lord. Even though You were angry with me, Your anger is turned away and You comfort me. See, God saves me. I will trust and not be afraid. For the Lord God is my strength and song. And He has become the One Who saves me."

Isaiah 12:1–2 NLV

I tell you the truth, you will weep and mourn over what is going to happen to me, but the world will rejoice. You will grieve, but your grief will suddenly turn to wonderful joy.

John 16:20 NLT

May all who come to you
 be glad and joyful.
May all who are thankful for your salvation
 always say, "How great is God!"

Psalm 70:4 GNT

You make the path of life known to me.
Complete joy is in your presence.
Pleasures are by your side forever.

Psalm 16:11 GW

NEW SONG

Dear Lord,

You are my strength and my shield.

What a joy that You help me as I trust in You. It's one more reason why I give thanks to You with my song of praise.

Never mind if I can't carry a tune; I will sing boldly and express my love to You. I will praise You with all my heart. I will tell about Your wonderful deeds as I sing You a new song, joining in with the beautiful voices of heavenly choirs.

For You are worthy to open the scroll and the seals to the hidden things that are to come.

You are worthy because You were slain, and Your blood purchased people of every tribe, nation, and tongue.

My voice joins a multitude of voices who praise You!

Thank You that I and my brothers and sisters in Christ belong to You.

Thank You for Your sacrifice on the cross for our sins.

"Sing for joy, O heavens! Be glad, O earth. Break out into songs of joy, O mountains." For the Lord comforted me. He has comforted His people. He has comforted us with His loving-pity whenever we suffer. He has saved us from our sins.

Thank You, Lord.

The LORD is my strength and my shield.
My heart trusted him, so I received help.
My heart is triumphant; I give thanks to him with my song.

Psalm 28:7 GW

Sing to Him a new song;
play each the best way you can,
and don't be afraid to be bold with your joyful feelings.

Psalm 33:3 VOICE

Sing to him; yes, sing his praises.
Tell everyone about his wonderful deeds.

Psalm 105:2 NLT

And they sang a new song, saying:

"You are worthy to take the scroll
and to open its seals,
because you were slain,
and with your blood you purchased for God
persons from every tribe and language and people
and nation."

Revelation 5:9 NIV

Sing for joy, O heavens! Be glad, O earth! Break out into songs of joy, O mountains! For the Lord has comforted His people. He will have loving-pity on His suffering people.

Isaiah 49:13 NLV

POWERFUL GOD

Dear Lord,

Sometimes I wonder how I, in my weakness, can serve You, the all-powerful God. Then I remember that Jesus Christ walked this earth in a frail human body. When He died on the cross, You resurrected Him back to life through Your mighty power.

I too live in a frail human body, but I'm alive with Christ through the power You have given me.

I admit I have spent much time thinking about Your strength as compared to my weakness. You say that Your grace is all I need and that Your power is greater in my weakness, and then I realize my weakness is a blessing that I can use to serve You. How happy I am that I'm weak, because this is how I partner with Your power operating in and through me. Therefore, I will be strong in Your strength because nothing is impossible for You.

I believe in Your mighty power. It is at work in me to accomplish possibilities greater than I could ever dream up. These possibilities will become reality because Your miraculous power is working in ways I can't even imagine.

What a joy to be empowered with Your power.

Thank You, Lord.

Christ's weak human body died on a cross. It is by God's power that Christ lives today. We are weak. We are as He was. But we will be alive with Christ through the power God has for us.

2 Corinthians 13:4 NLV

But his answer was: "My grace is all you need, for my power is greatest when you are weak." I am most happy, then, to be proud of my weaknesses, in order to feel the protection of Christ's power over me.

2 Corinthians 12:9 GNT

Be strong with the Lord's strength.

Ephesians 6:10 NLV

For nothing will be impossible with God.

Luke 1:37 ESV

Now to him who is able to do far more abundantly than all that we ask or think, according to the power at work within us.

Ephesians 3:20 ESV

POWERFUL WORD

Dear Lord,

I love Your Word. It's alive and active in and through Your Spirit. Your Word is sharper than any two-edged sword. It penetrates the point that separates soul from spirit and joints from marrow. Your Word judges the thoughts of my heart as well as my intentions.

Your Word is a lamp unto my feet, a light that cuts through the darkness and illuminates the path You have set before me.

The Word of the cross may seem ridiculous to those who are spiritually dying because of their sin, only because they haven't discovered its power. But because I know the power of the cross, I am saved from the price that must be paid as punishment for my sin. The cross introduces me to Your awesome love. It reveals the sacrifice a loving God would make for me.

May the lost hear this message of hope so that they too can be set free. May my loved ones hear and discover the power of the cross for themselves.

How happy I am that I've heard this message and have received the forgiveness of sin.

Because of the cross, I know the salvation You offer me through Jesus, and this good news has filled my life with joy.

Thank You, Lord.

Because God's word is living, active, and sharper than any two-edged sword. It penetrates to the point that it separates the soul from the spirit and the joints from the marrow. It's able to judge the heart's thoughts and intentions.

Hebrews 4:12 CEB

Your word is a lamp for my steps;
it lights the path before me.

Psalm 119:105 VOICE

For the word of the cross is folly to those who are perishing, but to us who are being saved it is the power of God.

1 Corinthians 1:18 ESV

Consequently, faith comes from hearing the message, and the message is heard through the word about Christ.

Romans 10:17 NIV

But he said, "Happy rather are those who hear God's word and put it into practice."

Luke 11:28 CEB

PRAISING GOD

Dear Lord,

I've learned that the solution to life's pain, hurts, and betrayals is when I can push past myself and into praising You.

My praise flips the script of my negative thoughts and changes my focus to You. It gives me a way to turn from my fears and trust in You. This is one more reason why I sing the glory of Your name and make my praise of You a celebration.

May my shouts of joy join with the shouts now arising from the whole earth.

You, the Eternal One, are my strength and my song. You have sent Jesus to come and save me. You are my God, and I will continue to praise You. You have been the God to the people who love You now and in generations past.

With my whole life, as well as my body, mind, and emotions and every part of who I am, I bow in wonder and love before You, Holy God. When You heal me, I am healed. When You save me, I am saved, for You are the One I praise.

May my joy arise as I worship You.

Thank You, Lord.

Shout for joy to God, all the earth!
Sing the glory of his name;
make his praise glorious.

Psalm 66:1–2 NIV

The Eternal is my strength and my song,
and He has come to save me;
He is my God, and I will praise Him.
He is the God of my father, and I will exalt Him.

Exodus 15:2 VOICE

O my soul, come, praise the Eternal
with all that is in me—body, emotions, mind, and will—every part of who I am—
praise His holy name.

Psalm 103:1 VOICE

Heal me, Lord, and I will be healed;
save me and I will be saved,
for you are the one I praise.

Jeremiah 17:14 NIV

PRESSING INTO GOD

Dear Lord,

Sometimes I trip over my struggles or get distracted by the everyday problems of life and forget to press into new levels of my faith, even beyond the basis of having faith in You and feeling sorry as I turn from my sins. But I do not want to forget You, the One who loves me, the One who has so much joy waiting for me.

So, I ask You to forgive me for all the times my thoughts did not turn to You when they should have.

I realize it's time to build on the foundation You laid before me so I can turn toward works that will embrace faith in You. It's time I push past my beginnings in Christ and advance toward perfection.

Perfection is a goal I haven't yet obtained, but even so, I'm pressing on to receive everything Jesus has in store for me. I will not let anything stand in my way because Jesus is with me.

Jesus once said that even if I have faith the size of a mustard seed, nothing will be impossible for me. So, by faith I can tell the mountains to move out of my way and they will.

I have a ways to go, but I'm doing this one thing right: I'm running to You, putting everything on the line for Your purposes for me. I'm sprinting toward the only goal that matters, my race to the finish line!

So, with joy I will run the race to win the prize to live forever with my Lord, Christ Jesus.

Thank You, Lord.

So let us leave the first things you need to know about Christ. Let us go on to the teaching that full-grown Christians should understand. We do not need to teach these first truths again. You already know that you must be sorry for your sins and turn from them. You know that you must have faith in God.

Hebrews 6:1 NLV

He told them, "Because you have so little faith. I can guarantee this truth: If your faith is the size of a mustard seed, you can say to this mountain, 'Move from here to there,' and it will move. Nothing will be impossible for you."

Matthew 17:20 GW

I'm not there yet, nor have I become perfect; but I am charging on to gain anything and everything the Anointed One, Jesus, has in store for me—and nothing will stand in my way because He has grabbed me and won't let me go. Brothers and sisters, as I said, I know I have not arrived; but there's one thing I am doing: I'm leaving my old life behind, putting everything on the line for this mission. I am sprinting toward the only goal that counts: to cross the line, to win the prize, and to hear God's call to resurrection life found exclusively in Jesus the Anointed.

Philippians 3:12–14 VOICE

REFLECTING ON GOD'S NAMES

Dear Lord,

You are a God of many names, names that describe You and tell of Your greatness. It's almost surprising that one of Your names is "Jealous." You are not jealous of me or of any of Your creations. Instead, You are jealous of my attention. You want me to seek You first, not my television, my favorite news station, or even Google. You want me to talk to You and keep You at the forefront of my thoughts. Help me to keep my focus on You.

You are "I AM WHO I AM." This means You are the most important force in the universe, the universe which You created. Help me to remember that You are forever present with me.

You are also "the First and the Last, the beginning and the end of all things . . . the All-powerful One Who was and Who is and Who is to come." You always were, You always will be. You are eternal and forever and always.

You sent Your Son, the Prince of Peace, as a child who was born for us. You loved us enough to send Your Son, a part of Your Godhead, to us. Your love is astounding.

You are the Good Shepherd, who gave Your life for the sheep so I could know You forever.

How joyful to know that my God—who is jealous of my attention and is loving, ever present, eternal, and forever and always God—sent His Son, the Good Shepherd, for me. What an amazing joy that I can know and spend my life with You.

Thank You, Lord.

Do not worship any other god, for the LORD, whose name is Jealous, is a jealous God.

Exodus 34:14 NIV

Eternal One: I AM WHO I AM. This is what you should tell the people of Israel: "I AM has sent me to rescue you."

Exodus 3:14 VOICE

The Lord God says, "I am the First and the Last, the beginning and the end of all things. I am the All-powerful One Who was and Who is and Who is to come."

Revelation 1:8 NLV

A child will be born for us.
A son will be given to us.
The government will rest on his shoulders.
He will be named:
Wonderful Counselor,
Mighty God,
Everlasting Father,
Prince of Peace.

Isaiah 9:6 GW

I am the good shepherd. The good shepherd gives his life for the sheep.

John 10:11 GW

RISE AND SHINE

Dear Lord,

I once stumbled in thick darkness, the same darkness that covers the nations and the earth. But one day the truth of who You are dawned into my heart and my life was filled with light.

You foretold that a light would shine out of darkness. This glory is cast by Your "Sun" of Righteousness, now revealed as Your Son, Christ Jesus. Jesus is the light of the world. He promised that if I follow Him, I will never walk in darkness but will have His light in my life.

And now the light of Christ shines into my heart with the knowledge of Your glory.

Jesus, who has risen with healing in His wings, shares His healing to all who fear His name.

Because I'm a carrier of Your light, You complete my soul as You heal my broken life. I leap with the joy of new life inside of me as I celebrate Your presence in me.

You ask that I shine this light, the glory of Your majesty, to others.

How can I hide it? With joy I will let Your light shine bright before everyone. When they see this light, they will glorify You!

Thank You, Lord.

Arise! Shine! Your light has come,
and the glory of the Lord has dawned.
Darkness now covers the earth,
and thick darkness covers the nations.
But the Lord dawns,
and his glory appears over you.

Isaiah 60:1–2 GW

The Sun of Righteousness will rise with healing in his wings for you people who fear my name. You will go out and leap like calves let out of a stall.

Malachi 4:2 GW

For God, who said, "Let light shine out of darkness," has shone in our hearts to give the light of the knowledge of the glory of God in the face of Jesus Christ.

2 Corinthians 4:6 ESV

When Jesus spoke again to the people, he said, "I am the light of the world. Whoever follows me will never walk in darkness, but will have the light of life."

John 8:12 NIV

In the same way, let your light shine before others, that they may see your good deeds and glorify your Father in heaven.

Matthew 5:16 NIV

SAVING GRACE

Dear Lord,

I was once lost, but You found me. I was once a prisoner of the evil one, but You freed me. I was once bound in chains, bound for hell, but You rescued me.

How can I fully celebrate this gift You have given me, this beautiful gift of grace that reveals the depth of Your love? This gift of grace offers the gift of salvation to all people, including me.

When Jesus came into the world, He was born as a gift of love from You to all people. When Jesus started His earthly ministry, He explained it this way: "I am the way, and the truth, and the life. No one comes to the Father except through me."

Jesus is our door to You, Lord, and through Him, You save us from punishment for our sins. This is a kindness that Jesus gave us. I have nothing to contribute to Your gift of salvation.

You explained, Lord, that even though I belong to You, You are the one who chose me, not the other way around. You chose me so I could bear everlasting fruit like love and kindness.

And as I live in Your love, loving You, loving others, You will give me whatever I ask in the name of Jesus.

You poured Your amazing grace on me, and I have been transformed to be who I am, one who produces fruit. This business of working in and through Your love is hard work, but even so, I do all You've called me to do, not in my own strength but in Yours.

Thank You, Lord.

We have cause to celebrate because the grace of God has appeared, offering the gift of salvation to all people.

Titus 2:11 VOICE

Jesus said to him, “I am the way, and the truth, and the life. No one comes to the Father except through me.”

John 14:6 ESV

God saved you through faith as an act of kindness. You had nothing to do with it. Being saved is a gift from God.

Ephesians 2:8 GW

You did not choose me; I chose you and appointed you to go and bear much fruit, the kind of fruit that endures. And so the Father will give you whatever you ask of him in my name.

John 15:16 GNT

But whatever I am now, it is all because God poured out his special favor on me—and not without results. For I have worked harder than any of the other apostles; yet it was not I but God who was working through me by his grace.

1 Corinthians 15:10 NLT

SOUL CLEANSING

Dear Lord,

How often I have misjudged You, thinking You were holding out on my promises. Instead, You were teaching me patience as you gracefully waited for me to turn to You, so to make things right between us.

You are a loving God, and You do not want anyone, including me, to endure punishment forever. You want the ones you love to repent and turn away from their sins and back to You.

How thankful I am that You are faithful and reliable. If I confess my sins to You, You forgive me and cleanse me from all that I've done wrong.

You call Your people to humble themselves before You. So, I humble myself now and lift my voice to join the chorus of those calling out to You. I seek Your face. I turn from my wicked ways. You respond by allowing me to hear from heaven while You forgive my sins and heal our land.

But the most important thing I can do is lay my soul bare before You and ask, like King David did when he repented of his sin, that You purify my heart and make my spirit steadfast and new. Keep me always in Your presence, always filled with Your Holy Spirit.

Lord, I will practice the joy of Your saving power as You give me the ability to obey You. You will empower me to shine Your light to those living in darkness. When they see You are the source of the light, they will turn from their sins and follow after You.

Thank You, Lord.

The Lord is not slow about keeping His promise as some people think. He is waiting for you. The Lord does not want any person to be punished forever. He wants all people to be sorry for their sins and turn from them.

2 Peter 3:9 NLV

God is faithful and reliable. If we confess our sins, he forgives them and cleanses us from everything we've done wrong.

1 John 1:9 GW

If my people who are called by my name humble themselves, and pray and seek my face and turn from their wicked ways, then I will hear from heaven and will forgive their sin and heal their land.

2 Chronicles 7:14 ESV

Make a clean heart in me, O God. Give me a new spirit that will not be moved. Do not throw me away from where You are. And do not take Your Holy Spirit from me. Let the joy of Your saving power return to me. And give me a willing spirit to obey you. Then I will teach wrong-doers Your ways. And sinners will turn to You.

Psalm 51:10–13 NLV

WORSHIPING GOD IN SPIRIT AND TRUTH

Dear Lord,

When the woman at the well met Jesus, He revealed that He already knew her, and though they'd never met, Jesus told her everything she'd ever done. He even shared a mystery about a coming hour, an hour now here, when true worshipers will worship You in both spirit and truth. You seek these worshipers.

I, for one, volunteer to be such a worshiper. For You, God, are Spirit. I worship You through Your Spirit with my spirit, in the truth of who You are and the truth of what Christ Jesus did for me.

For You are near to all who call on You, to all who call on You in truth. I call You now, breathing in Your Spirit. I see that I must turn away from my sins.

I would rejoice in the privilege to be baptized in the name of Jesus. For baptism represents that I have died and been resurrected with Christ. May my sins be forgiven so I will receive the gift of the presence of the Holy Spirit. For You give me Your Spirit as proof that I live in You and You live in me.

It's a beautiful miracle that You, the God who created the universe, the God who dwells in me, allow me to become a temple of Your presence. With You filling my heart and soul, how can I not worship You?

You are so dear, and I love You so much. Your presence and Your truth give me joy.

Thank You, Lord.

But the hour is coming, and is now here, when the true worshipers will worship the Father in spirit and truth, for the Father is seeking such people to worship him.

John 4:23 ESV

God is Spirit. Those who worship Him must worship Him in spirit and in truth.

John 4:24 NLV

The Lord is near to all who call on him,
to all who call on him in truth.

Psalm 145:18 NIV

Peter said to them, "Each one of you must turn away from your sins and be baptized in the name of Jesus Christ, so that your sins will be forgiven; and you will receive God's gift, the Holy Spirit."

Acts 2:38 GNT

And God has given us his Spirit as proof that we live in him and he in us.

1 John 4:13 NLT

CONCLUSION

> Dear friends, your faith is going to be tested as if it were going through fire. Do not be surprised at this. Be happy that you are able to share some of the suffering of Christ. When His shining-greatness is shown, you will be filled with much joy. If men speak bad of you because you are a Christian, you will be happy because the Spirit of shining-greatness and of God is in you.
>
> 1 Peter 4:12–14 NLV

I always anticipate the way God leads me to personally experience whatever topic I'm writing about. So, I was especially pleased that I would be writing about joy! I expected laughter and happiness to surround me.

But God showed me that the road to joy can come through trials. How happy I was to have these great Scriptures and Scripture-based prayers as I faced a fiery battle. The Word-based prayers sustained me and allowed me to stay joyful as I watched God move on my behalf.

Now it's your turn. Don't be afraid of the fiery trials ahead because God is going to use them not only to bring you closer to Him but to get you through your circumstances as He turns your difficulties into blessings. I am a witness!

Pray with me!

Dear Lord,

Thank You for the time I shared with You as I prayed through this book.

It helped. It changed my perspective. It brought me joy.

While I'm still traveling earthly roads filled with pain, I thank You for the privilege of sharing Your suffering. For as I do, Your love shines in and through me and fills me with unquenchable joy. Even if people misunderstand the love we share, I'm so grateful that You call me Yours.

These trials I face here on earth allow Your Holy Spirit to shine through me as a light that not only guides me but also guides people to You. One day You will call me home, where You will wipe away my every tear. But for now, I press on with You in the power of Your love and in Your beautiful gift of joy.

Thank You, Lord.

ACKNOWLEDGMENTS

Special thanks to all my friends who prayed and walked with me, especially my dear friends Karen Porter and Joy Schneider; and my team, Rebecca White, Carla Wicks, and Amber Weigand-Buckley; as well as my nonprofit board and steering members. They loved me and fought the good fight by my side, encouraging me when I needed it most. Also, thanks to my editors, Vicki Crumpton and Kristin Adkinson, and the wonderful team at Revell of Baker Publishing Group; my brilliant agent, Janet Kobobel Grant; and my dear family members, who lend me their patience and support as I write book after book. I am so thankful for the thousand women of the Advanced Writers and Speakers Association, my team of prayer warriors who continue to pray for me. I love you all! And, of course, a special thanks to my Lord and Savior, Jesus Christ. He is my joy.

ABOUT THE AUTHOR

Linda Evans Shepherd is an award-winning author of thirty-eight books, including the bestselling *When You Don't Know What to Pray*, as well as *When You Need to Move a Mountain*, *Praying through Every Emotion*, and *Prayers for Every Need*.

Linda is an internationally recognized speaker and has spoken across the United States and around the world.

She is the CEO of Right to the Heart Ministries and founded the Advanced Writers and Speakers Association (AWSA), which ministers to Christian women authors and speakers (www.AWSA.com). She is also the publisher of their complimentary *Leading Hearts* magazine for women (www.LeadingHearts.com) as well as Arise Daily (www.AriseDaily.com), a free daily e-devotional. She is the founder of Arise Esther, LLC (www.AriseEsther.com). Linda loves to hang out with her friends, family, and hubby, Paul. She is the mother of two wonderful kids, one in Austin and the other in heaven.

Visit Linda and hear her prayers and prayer stories on her Pray with Linda YouTube channel (www.PrayYouTube.com), and follow her on Twitter @LindaShepherd or on Facebook @LindaEvansShepherdAuthor.

To learn more about Linda's books, go to www.GotToPray.com.

Linda has created a downloadable gift for you called "21 Secrets to a Joyful Heart Checklist." To get your free copy, go to www.JoyfulHeartSecrets.com.

Transform Your Life through Prayer with Linda Evans Shepherd

Visit **GotToPray.com** to receive a FREE prayer toolbox, find printable prayers, submit a prayer request, and learn more about Linda's SPEAKING and BLOGGING.

Linda Evans Shepherd

 @LindaShepherd

Linda Evans Shepherd

Linda Evans Shepherd

Find a Prayer for Every Stage of Life